Perfect Phrases™ for Writing Employee Surveys

Hundreds of Ready-to-Use Phrases to Help You Create Surveys Your Employees Answer Honestly, Completely, and Helpfully

John Kador
Katherine J. Armstrong

New York Chicago San Francisco Lisbon
London Madrid Mexico City Milan New Delhi
San Juan Seoul Singapore Sydney Toronto

The McGraw·Hill Companies

1 2 3 4 5 6 7 8 9 0   WFR/WFR   1 5 4 3 2 1 0

ISBN: 978-0-07-166401-1
MHID: 0-07-166401-7

McGraw-Hill books are available at special quantity discounts to use as premiums and sales promotions, or for use in corporate training programs. To contact a representative please visit the Contact Us pages at www.mhprofessional.com.

Contents

Contents

Chapter 4: Putting It Together   19

Part Two: Perfect Phrases   41

Chapter 5: Setting the Stage   43

Contents

Chapter 6:   Employee Satisfaction and Engagement Surveys   55

Contents

Chapter 7: Leadership and Management   73

Contents

Chapter 8: Values and Ethics   85

Contents

Chapter 9: Aspects of Organizational Culture 97

Chapter 10: Work Environment 109

Contents

Contents

Chapter 12: Performance, Career Development, and Training 129

Contents

Contents

Chapter 15: Information Technology   159

Chapter 16: Internal Communications   163

Chapter 17: Alternative Survey Approaches   171

Contents

Contents

Acknowledgments

We would like to acknowledge the enormous help given to us in creating this book. This book represents the experience, wisdom, and attention of dozens of professionals. For their trust, their patience, and their guidance, we thank the experts and practitioners interviewed for this book who confirmed what we knew and introduced us to new ideas. The examples of the employee surveys they entrusted to us are included in this book as a testament to their willingness to help others and develop the art of this important organizational tool.

Perhaps the best preparation for writing this book has been the time we have spent in organizations small and large, public and private, for and not-for profit. We thank, therefore, all of the clients and colleagues we have had over the years who have taught us how to help employees find their voice and how to help management demonstrate openness to listening. In particular, Katherine would like to thank her clients and friends at Volac—James Neville, Andy Richardson and Stuart Garrick—for their confidence over the years and for specific input into this book. John thanks Diane Asyre for her many contributions and courtesies.

Thanks go also to Emily Carleton at McGraw-Hill for reaching out to us to write this book. Emily and her colleagues at McGraw-Hill streamlined and supported this project from start to finish, and we thank them for their professionalism and efficiency.

Acknowledgments

With a summer deadline, this book was not completed in the winter weekday work hours usually invisible to our families. To Anna Beth, Rachel, and Dan; and to Rob, Megan, and Caroline, thank you for your patience and sacrifice. We will somehow make it up to you.

This book is dedicated to:

My son, Daniel
—John

My husband, Rob
—Katherine

Introduction
Leadership Means
Listening and Learning

An employee survey begins a conversation. It's an opportunity to display serious leadership though listening.

Effective employee surveys give your leadership team the opportunity to listen accurately, objectively, fairly, and quickly to dozens, hundreds, or even thousands of employees at the same time—to learn about their experience at work, their ideas and, perhaps most important, their opinion about the quality of your leadership team. The learning—and the action that flows from the learning—justifies the time and expense that goes into designing, implementing, and analyzing the survey.

This book will help you with all three steps of the survey process, especially in the design phase, in which you decide what questions to ask and how to phrase them. Many survey projects lose their way because of the wording of survey items. This book provides hundreds of proven questions for dozens of the most popular survey applications. All the phrases in the book have been vetted. That is, they have been used in successful surveys by organizations like yours. If you use the perfect phrases suggested in this book as the basis for your own application, your survey will escape many of the traps and pitfalls that can undermine your efforts.

Introduction

A well-conducted employee survey will give you actionable data to structure initiatives, evaluate ongoing and completed projects, and contemplate future action. A survey can help you allocate resources, map your future, and strengthen your bottom line. You'll be able to gauge employee satisfaction, create internal policies, and lower turnover. But there's an even greater reason to survey employees: when implemented correctly, employee surveys introduce a process that not only generates reliable learning but also increases employee engagement, commitment, and loyalty.

In the past, many companies have been reluctant to conduct surveys because the process was cumbersome, time-consuming, and expensive. In the days before Web-based tools, mounting a survey was indeed a major chore involving significant expenses for printing, administration, data entry, and analysis. The good news is that most of these objections have gone the way of the printed employee magazine. New services have automated almost every step of the survey process. Everything is online and Web-based, eliminating much of the time, tedium, and cost of the old paper-based processes. All knowledge workers have access to computers, and even most hourly employees know how to fill out a survey on a computer. Best of all, these services are absolutely free for simple surveys.

Just One Little Problem

Someone has to actually write the questions and the other parts of the survey package. And if you're reading this book, we guess that someone is you. Relax. This book is going to make writing the survey components easy. We're going to give you models for introducing the survey process. We will provide the language for the survey instructions. We're going to give you the exact wording and scales for all the questions you need to ask. And we're going to give you organization-tested, effective follow-up language that will transform your surveys into action plans and powerful employee engagement.

That follow-up step is absolutely critical. Employees welcome participating in surveys when they have confidence that the views they express will be part of a thoughtful management process that will lead to action that is in their interest. They can be confident of the leadership team's openness only if there's some kind of acknowledgment of the input they've given. Follow-up is what transforms a survey from rote process to active listening. As long as you and your leadership team are truly committed to active listening, you'll build among employees

- Awareness of the issues management is dealing with and the language the organization is using
- Deeper understanding of the goals and values of the organization
- More considered and complete definitions of success
- A powerful and efficient upstream communication channel you'll be able to use again and again
- Understanding that measurement is part of your organization's commitment to continuous learning
- Confidence that their views are important to the success of the organization
- Engagement with an organization that involves them in decision making

Perfect Phrases

In keeping with other books in the Perfect Phrases series, most of the content of this book consists of hundreds of tested perfect phrases for all steps of the employee survey process. Part Two organizes these perfect phrases for the actual survey items—questions and statements as well as supporting phrases, instructions, announcements, and thank you letters—into dozens of categories. Whatever your survey requirements, you are likely to find what you need. Take a look at the Contents to find the precise category you're looking for. You'll find survey items to ascertain employees' understanding and commitment to the vision, values, mission, and culture of the organization. You'll also find items to navigate the sensitive subject of asking for honest feedback about management performance. We include a number of employee satisfaction and engagement surveys. Rounding out the lists are sample surveys from actual organizations that gather employee opinions to improve processes and drive success.

Do It Yourself

With the help of this book, there is no reason you cannot implement a thoroughly professional employee survey by yourself, in one day, at no cost. Web-based platforms for conducting employee surveys are that sophisticated, flexible, and easy to use. On the other hand, there are some limitations to what you can do yourself. For example, some employee surveys need to guarantee anonymity to participants in order to get totally honest results. In such a case, we recommend entrusting the survey to an external partner. And, in all cases, we recommend you reach out to trusted colleagues to assist you with the survey, taking the time necessary to build awareness and pretest your prototype. Just because technology makes it easy to implement an employee survey by yourself in one day is no reason you should.

You may need additional resources on other occasions. The survey you need may be larger and more complicated than the free tools can handle. Maybe the up-front planning and survey design require expertise that you don't have. Or, on the back end, you may need more complicated analytical and reporting tools than the free services provide. Chapters 4 and 20 give tips about bringing in outside Web-based survey platforms, design firms, analytical and reporting partners, and consulting firms that can extend your capabilities.

Employee surveys can be a catalyst for organizational improvement, innovation, and even transformation. You begin simply by using the right words. Let's get started.

Part One

Before you begin writing the actual survey, consider the whole process and what you'll need to do to bring others—both management and employees—on board. This part of the book lays out a path from start to finish and shares advice from practitioners who've learned, sometimes the hard way, what works and what doesn't.

Chapter 1
Know What You're Getting Into

S tart by considering the five main tasks that make up an effective
employee survey process:

1. Define the goals of the survey. Determine whom you want to
   learn from, why you want that learning, and what precise
   information you seek. Why survey at all? Chapter 2 is your guide to
   survey definition.
2. Set reasonable expectations. Prepare the landscape with both
   management and employees before the survey to ensure that
   everyone is on the same page regarding the goals of the survey
   and how the resulting information will be used. Chapter 3 gives
   more detail about this step.
3. Design the survey. This step is like outlining a document before
   writing. Make a list of the main parts of the survey and their order,
   determine survey techniques you want to use, and select your
   administration method. Chapter 4 gives an overview of the
   decisions you'll need to make and common mistakes to avoid.
4. Write the survey. Part Two (Chapters 5–19) gives you easy access
   to hundreds of sample questions, sorted by the specific kind of
   survey you are conducting, plus ideas for introductory and
   concluding language.

5. Collect, analyze, and communicate the results, not just to the management team but also to the employees who were surveyed. Part Three focuses on how to share the findings so that management can not only act on the results but also draw the link between changes and the survey.

Employee surveys can fail at any point in the process as a result of objectives that are not clear; poor design in the process; ineffective questions; mistakes in administration (a survey that is too long, sent at the wrong time, or sent to the wrong people); a low or uneven response rate; faulty analysis of the data; and, quite frequently, in the actions taken or not taken based on the survey data.

To avoid these pitfalls, give yourself enough time to think through each of the steps. Keep in mind that your first survey will take longer to plan than subsequent ones. Two processes are going to eat up time in the planning phase. The first is learning, and the second is consensus building. To jump-start your learning, talk to colleagues to see if they have relevant communications or analytical expertise. Trone, a marketing communications firm based in North Carolina, turned to its Ph.D. statisticians to design the first survey for its own employees. Trone has adapted consumer research methodology to surveying employee satisfaction based on the net number of staff who would recommend the company as an employer.

You don't have to do it by yourself, and that doesn't necessarily mean engaging outside consultants. You may have all the resources you need right in your own organization. If your company sells a product or service, it probably has a marketing department that knows its way around surveys. Your finance or accounting department probably has statisticians or folks who love to crunch numbers. Members of your IT department may be able to install and troubleshoot Web-based and off-the-shelf survey tools. Ask for help appropriately and early, and they'll stick with you. Run to them late in the process with urgent demands, and you're likely to meet resistance. By asking colleagues to be on a short-term task force or even just for their ideas, you'll shorten your learning curve and build consensus at the same time. The very act of asking for help builds awareness and ultimately spreads ownership of the employee survey process deeper into the organization.

Perfect Phrases for Asking for Help

- I'm planning an employee survey process and I know you have some experience in [field of expertise] that could be useful. Could we schedule a 15-minute conversation so that I can learn more about what specific expertise you have that could help make this process more effective?
- I'm putting together a short-term task force to design the process for our next employee survey. Are you available to join? I estimate it will involve [number] meetings or conference calls over the next [number] weeks.
- Your expertise would be invaluable in an employee survey I'm planning.
- We have an opportunity to gain some important information by surveying the employees on [subject]. Can I meet with you to get your input so we can design and implement the best survey possible?

To save time on future surveys, be sure to document your process as you go along. After each step, take a few minutes to debrief and note what went well and what didn't. Once you have the process down, you'll be able to conduct frequent, short surveys to keep your information up to date and your employees reminded of their value to the organization.

Chapter 2
Defining Survey Goals

Before you can design the survey, it's important to ask, "Why survey at all?" Organizations conduct surveys to discover answers to certain questions, but perhaps there are other ways to get the information your organization needs. Surveys are best for asking questions to which you genuinely don't know the answer. So before you go through the trouble of doing a survey, ask yourself if anyone else in the organization possibly has the answers to the questions already.

You'll be tempted to begin a survey by writing the questions. This approach is a mistake and will set you back. If you begin by writing the questions, you'll lose focus on what's important.

Unless the goal of the survey is to gather general baseline information about employee attitudes, the most effective employee surveys tend to be focused on one or two narrow issues or topics about which decisions need to be made. When the results allow the organization to make a more informed decision about these matters, the survey has served its purpose. To get to that point, you'll need as many employees as possible to respond completely, honestly, and promptly. Chapter 4 includes many hints for increasing participation and reliability rates.

Summarize Your Goals

Many organizations find it helpful to begin by encapsulating their survey goals in broad terms by completing the following summary statements:

We will conduct an employee survey ...
- To listen to _____ in order
- to learn _____ and/or
- to quantify _____.

Notice that the first blank encourages you to define *which* employees will be surveyed. The second focuses you on learning, and the third lays out what data you need in order to make decisions.

Experienced survey designers always begin by committing the research goals to writing. Clearly stated goals keep a research project focused. There are as many survey goal statements as there are surveys. The Perfect Phrases box that follows offers a number of questions that can be inserted in the "to learn" or "to quantify" fields in the rubric. They can help guide you in creating a unique statement for your own survey.

Here are a few examples of how this rubric can work:

We will conduct an employee survey ...
- To listen to <u>all employees</u> in order
- to learn <u>about their sense of satisfaction</u> and
- to quantify <u>any differences between sites</u>.

We will conduct an employee survey ...
- To listen to <u>new employees</u> in order
- to learn about <u>their early experience in our company</u> and
- to quantify <u>the effectiveness of our orientation programs</u>.

Perfect Phrases for Defining the Question

- How satisfied are new employees after 30 days on the job?
- Are employees satisfied with the career development opportunities the company offers?
- Is the mix of benefits the company currently offers contributing to employee satisfaction?
- Are there some benefits our employees would want the company to offer?
- What do our employees think of the service they are offering customers?
- Is there anything the company can do to keep valued employees from resigning?
- How effectively have the employees internalized the values the company promotes?
- What can the company do to promote employee collaboration?
- Are employees satisfied with the supervision they are receiving?
- Do employees think they have the right resources and tools to be productive?
- Is there a significant difference between the engagement of employees at facility A and employees in facility B?
- Are we doing enough of the right things to keep our employees satisfied and motivated?

Every survey needs to be a specific response to a specific question or set of related questions, the more specific the better. Regardless of your budget or the resources you have available, the survey process always begins with the end in mind. What question do you want to answer? What problem do you want to solve? What actions are your leaders willing to take in response to a survey?

Five Good Reasons for Conducting Surveys

1. **To discover what employees are thinking and doing.** In a nonthreatening survey environment, your organization will learn about what motivates employees, what's important to them, and how they actually behave.
2. **To prioritize the organization's actions based on objective data.** Rather than relying on subjective information or best guesses, you can gather objective information to make sound, data-driven decisions to help allocate scare resources.
3. **To provide a benchmark.** Surveying provides a snapshot of the employees and their attitudes about your survey problem at a certain point in time. This benchmark helps you establish a baseline from which you can compare whether attitudes and perceptions relative to the survey problem improve or worsen over time.
4. **To communicate the importance of key topics to employees.** Communicating with employees about the survey topic allows for deeper insights into the survey problem and signals the organization's eagerness to listen to employees and act on their concerns.
5. **To collect the combined brainpower and ideas of the workforce.** Employees have different perspectives than management yet sometimes cannot find or do not have access to a way to communicate those perspectives. Access their knowledge to improve decision making, overcome challenges, and seize opportunities.

Two Bad Reasons to Conduct a Survey

1. **To sell employees an idea.** Some organizations use a communication technique referred to as "push polling." A push

poll looks like a survey, but the questions guide the respondent down a path to a specified conclusion. If you are designing a survey with the goal of convincing employees of a certain point of view, you're not focused on learning or listening. A survey isn't the right tool for you.

2. **To solve problems in one easy step.** A survey is a means to an end, not an end in itself. It's simply disrespectful to put out a survey and think you've done all you need to address morale or productivity issues. In fact, a survey isolated from other communications and actions could be more detrimental than helpful because a survey generates not only information but also expectations. The very act of surveying employees builds the expectation that there will be some changes that will improve their experience. See Chapter 3 for more about setting and handling these expectations.

Communicate within the Organization

Communication is very important with colleagues during the design phase. Enlist help now and you might get some feedback that will impact the design of the survey. See the following box for perfect phrases you can use to communicate design goals.

Perfect Phrases to Communicate Survey Goals

This survey ...

- is essential to facilitating development and organizational change
- signals to employees that management is committed to change

---

- allows the organization to focus on needs and leverage its strengths
- informs the organization on which actions may create problems for employees
- helps the organization identify inefficiencies
- provides management with employee feedback (both positive and negative) on the internal health of the organization
- measures the impact of current programs, policies, and procedures
- helps the organization allocate scare resources for maximum effectiveness
- can be used to motivate employees and improve job satisfaction

Chapter 3
Setting Expectations

A ll surveys generate data. Effective surveys generate actionable information. That is, they yield insights that can be translated into action. If an organization cannot make a direct link between the survey and some eventual action, it may as well not conduct the survey. Employees are justifiably demoralized when they conclude that their employer thinks so little of their opinions. They would rather the organization be honest and not go through the pretense of asking employees what they think. The bottom line: know that your management team is open to take action of some kind before you begin.

Achieving this presurvey confidence may take more time and energy than any other aspect of the survey process. Practitioners agree that it really is the make-or-break step. John Frehse of Core Practice LLC, a consultancy that specializes in scheduling shift work and surveys employees for each project, spends a significant amount of time with management before each survey to describe the issues it will address. His team works with executives to understand the business and come up with up to a dozen options for improving workforce efficiency. Before these options go to employees in the form of a survey, Frehse makes certain that management is willing to accept, fund, and implement every one of the options if the survey results support it. If an option is off the table for management, it's not proposed to employees. There's no opportunity for management to backpedal. His advice: "Manage expectations every second of the day. We lay hot-button issues right out on the table and talk about how they will shape the coming weeks. Management has to know and agree up front about every aspect of the survey process. If they don't, we don't move forward with the survey. It's as simple as that."

Executive coach and organizational development consultant Leila Bulling Towne agrees: "I gain their commitment to action before conducting any employee survey. You have to know they are willing to do something based on the feedback." And what if that feedback ends up being about their personal performance? "Powerful employee surveys often expose weaknesses in the management team or in individual leadership performance," says Bulling Towne. "I make sure that the top people know they may hear some tough stuff." How does she prepare them for what may end up being a shock? "Before the survey," she explains, "I talk to individual clients about how the survey will speak to their personal credibility. I encourage them to be introspective before they have that external input. I'll ask, 'What do you think are the challenges to your personal credibility right now?' This one-on-one work opens the door for personal change based on employee survey feedback."

Kevin Murphy, managing partner at the marketing communications firm Trone, says that before an employee survey, the partners agree together about the survey process and their openness to action. They talk explicitly about how they are going to follow up with employees to learn more about the issues raised in a survey. "We have agreement around our table before we go any further," says Murphy. "We know we'll be busy and will need to be great listeners. We make that commitment before we start."

Bulling Towne has found that the more highly educated or metropolitan the workforce, the higher the expectations that management will actually follow through on their input. While that high level of expectation can be daunting, the flipside is that this employee population is more likely to complete the survey.

Difficult Conversations

We know it's difficult to have these conversations with upper management. Consider three strategies. First, try to begin and end the conversation with the potential impact on business results and the bottom line. Making that link explicit can break down all kinds of communications barriers. Second, start with a limited, closed-ended survey that doesn't leave the door open for out-of-the-blue options or personal feedback to management. You won't generate insights that are as deep, but you'll build comfort with and awareness of the process. Third, consider bringing in a consultant, facilitator, or coach. An outsider usually brings a sense of safety, objectivity, and credibility that increases transparency and action. Remember that you can bring in resources for just one part of the process and still do the rest yourself.

It's not just about raising the expectation for action. It's also about *limiting* management's expectation about the power of one survey. Employee surveys are *part* of the solution to problems, not the only tool you'll need. While a regular commitment to well-designed employee surveys contributes to employee engagement, one survey alone, no matter how good, isn't going to turn around a history of disengagement. Employees have great insight because they are often closer to customers, products, and processes than management, but they often aren't exposed to the big picture that links ideas together. Their input may need to be titrated with a broader view of the business. And brace your management team for inconsistencies across the organization. The singular "staff" is made of hundreds or thousands or tens of thousands of individuals. You may end up hearing a cacophony of voices instead of one "employee" voice. Let management know that the message may not be clear and that they may have to let down some staff when they respond to others.

Preparing Employees

Once management has bought into taking action based on the survey feedback, turn your attention to preparing the employee landscape. You're working on two levels here. You need to know and plan for how the actual survey will be perceived by staff. And you need to clarify what level of action and change is possible after the survey.

Let's start with understanding the soil into which the seeds of your survey will be sown. Are employees likely to respond? Will they take it seriously? Is there an emotional undercurrent that has the potential to capsize the survey process? At Cambridge, England, based dairy nutrition company Volac, communications manager Andy Richardson adds a step between defining survey goals and designing the survey process. Because employee surveys have not been part of this small, family-run private company, he or someone else sits down individually with a handful of employees to get the scoop on a particular issue involved in the survey. "Not only do I learn about what staff is thinking," says Richardson, "I also have the opportunity to curtail misunderstandings. It's an important step that gives me good information for designing the survey and communicating with management about employee feelings."

Remember that these premeetings not only give you information but also send a signal that you're listening. Choose participants carefully. It's not just about spreading the meetings across divisions, departments, or hierarchical levels. It's also about identifying and using internal opinion leaders. You know who these colleagues are: the ones who talk to everyone, who always have the latest scuttlebutt, who know who's on vacation, who speak up at meetings. Use their network to learn about how a survey is likely to be perceived and what issues need to be in it. Turn them into your ambassadors to generate excitement and credibility about the survey.

The other important prework with employees is sending the signal about the level of action that will be taken based on survey results. Surveying employees about their views of benefits packages? Let them know that a goal is to reduce cost and improve satisfaction by eliminating benefits that aren't popular and replacing them with improved options for benefits that are. Asking about ideas for innovation? Tell them you have resources to pursue just the two most promising ideas out of the hundreds that will be proposed, and let them know how that determination will be made.

Insists Core Practice's Frehse: "Be clear that you're only going to ask about options that are truly on the table. We work through and accept the business implications of an option before we propose it to employees. That way, we can assure them before the survey that any option they support is definitely an option for management."

Use both formal (blast e-mails, memos, remarks by executives) and informal (water cooler conversations with identified opinion leaders) communication vehicles to clarify what may happen after the survey.

At this point, you are almost ready to start writing the questions. Before you do, consider the design tips in Chapter 4.

From the Field

Core Practice's Frehse summarizes his tips for setting presurvey expectations as follows:

1. Always be open and honest about the purpose of the survey. If you aren't, it will hurt the effectiveness of the process.
2. Share as many pertinent details as possible with the employees so they know that their feedback is important.
3. Let employees know that they will see the results in a timely fashion. Share the feedback date with them and stick to it.

4. Always answer questions and take extra time offline with employees as required.
5. Set expectations around the impact of the survey. Let employees know that it won't establish mandates but will help management make better decisions.
6. Don't set the expectation that employees will get everything they want based on the results.

Chapter 4
Putting It Together

I n some ways it would be great if you could execute the survey by yourself, but please don't. As mentioned in Chapter 1, the survey will be better served if you invite a number of people to help you with the design, implementation, and data analysis. A survey project with a number of well-placed "owners" has a better shot at being successful. People with an investment in a project tend to give it priority. Orphan surveys—surveys that are perceived to be isolated projects of isolated managers—tend to be ignored.

Together, your team will need to make a number of decisions. In many cases, decisions are not a matter of right or wrong but a matter of trade-offs. With option A, you get one thing but give up another. With option B, the reverse is true. One person has a very hard time thinking through the issues. That's why you need teammates who have made an investment of time and energy. A committee or task force will help you think through the implications of each decision, help you put a survey together, and then promote the survey to encourage maximum participation.

What should you expect in terms of participation? Many smaller companies aim for 100 percent participation. That level is unlikely in a larger organization made of disparate units. Caren Goldberg, an HR professor at American University and consultant, has found that few surveys have response rates above 25 to 30 percent. She cautions that if you achieve much less than 20 percent, you need to be concerned about whether the 20 percent who responded are truly representative of the other 80 percent who didn't. In her experience, the highest response rates are on surveys conducted by researchers at academic institutions or those in which respondents are asked in person to complete the survey. As a practical matter, she notes, that one-on-one approach is not always possible.

The survey process decisions you make will have an impact on participation rates. Some of the most important involve:

- Timing: when should a survey go out, and how often?
- Length: how long is the survey?
- Sample size: who receives the survey?
- Anonymity: will responses be confidential or individually identified?
- Demographics: what basic personal information will you ask the respondent to provide?
- Incentives: what prizes are there for participation, if any?
- Online surveys: can you take advantage of easy electronic survey packages?
- Time frame for responses: how long do you give people to respond, and when do you send a reminder?
- Response formats: what kinds of scales will be provided for respondents to give their answers?

Timing Is Everything

Surveys come in two broad varieties: calendared surveys and needs-driven surveys.

Calendared Surveys

Organizations benefit from scheduled surveys. These surveys are released at preset times and provide predictability, continuity, and benchmark data. Though many organizations survey all or most employees every year, others survey only every two years. In turbulent times, some organizations move to shorter surveys every six months.

If you are now selecting your regular survey time, keep in mind any seasonality of your activity and processes. Employees in retail businesses, for instance, will be pressed for time around the holidays and may not appreciate the added task of filling out a survey. Many administrative people—from those in the finance department to those in marketing, sales, and production planning—won't want to take time to complete a survey during the budget season. In the summer, many employees are on vacation, and organizations tend to slow down. That may not be a good time to get a good read, either. Dairy nutrition company Volac's communications manager, Andy Richardson, explains that they conduct surveys in the autumn because people are in a thoughtful, back-to-business mentality that encourages participation.

Very large organizations such as Johnson & Johnson have so many employees around the world that different locations are surveyed on a rotating basis, with the core survey being conducted somewhere in the world each month.

Needs-Driven Surveys

Sometimes organizations need a one-off or ad hoc survey to give managers actionable information on a specific problem, challenge, or opportunity. These surveys take a temperature read of the organization when needed. You may find, then, that it's perfect to survey your employees during their busiest periods, because that's when they are more tuned in to stressors in their jobs and in operations. Likewise, you may conduct a survey within the month after a layoff in order to touch base with the remaining employees.

Every needs-driven survey exists in time. A survey about ideas for the summer picnic should probably come out in the late spring. A survey asking new hires about their experiences within their first 30 days should come right after their thirtieth day on the job.

Keep It Short

Length matters. In general, the shorter the survey, the better. Keep in mind that the employees you are surveying are just as busy as you are. A survey that asks unnecessary questions will take employees away from their work for longer than necessary and will reduce the number who complete the survey. The best way to cut your survey length is to make sure all questions are relevant to the goal question you want to answer. For instance, unless the survey is confidential, you already know the employee's gender, level, and work group, so you don't need to ask those questions again.

The recommended number of questions varies, in part based on your goal, survey frequency, and the type of survey question used. If your goal is to gauge employee opinion about the new parking lot, you want a very short survey. If you are conducting an extensive employee satisfaction or engagement survey in order to adjust your culture, policies, procedures, or structure, a longer survey is in order.

Likewise, if you like to survey employees each month on a specific topic, you'll want very short surveys indeed. But if you limit yourself to one calendared survey every two years, it's fine to ask an extensive number of questions. Another approach is to send out a relatively short general satisfaction or engagement survey (as covered in Chapter 6) and then one or two short follow-up surveys probing more deeply into areas that showed up as concerns or opportunities within the results of the general survey; Chapters 7 through 18 provide material for those secondary surveys.

Multiple-choice questions are quick to answer. Ranked and open-ended questions require more respondent—and analyst—time. A survey consisting entirely of questions that require open-ended responses should have fewer questions than a survey consisting entirely of multiple-choice questions. To limit overwhelmingly long answers to open-ended questions, design the online form to limit the number of characters a respondent can use for a response.

Expert opinions about the optimal length for a survey vary. Beeliner Surveys CEO Amanda Trombley encourages clients to keep surveys under 20 questions. Opinions Incorporated, a full-service opinion research organization that produces and administers customized surveys, suggests no more than 48 questions total. Yet many successful yearly surveys approach 100 questions or more. You know your environment: decide on the length that balances your need for information with the time and attention constraints of your employees.

Make sure you take the survey yourself. Better yet, ask a few colleagues to take it and time how long it takes. Put yourself in your target audience's shoes—could they realistically fit the survey into a busy day? If not, you risk losing participation.

Sample Sizes

There are two kinds of survey samples. A universal survey includes every member of the selected group, whether that is all employees, all shift workers, all female employees, or all U.S.-based employees, for instance. The other type is a random sample survey, which goes to a representative sample of employees. In theory, if the selection of participants is indeed random and the sample size is large enough, the results will be valid and the administration of the survey will be less cumbersome and expensive. But that's a big "if." Assuring that a survey is indeed random adds an order of statistical complexity that is outside the scope of this book. A downside of random sample surveys is that those employees not chosen may feel that their voices aren't heard and that they are not important. Since a very productive secondary effect of the survey process is building connection and understanding through this listening process, we suggest that you use universal surveys whenever at all feasible.

Anonymous Surveys

In other words, we're talking about confidentiality. In some surveys, the employee identifies himself or herself by name or employee identification number. In others, the employee is specifically promised that management will not know which employee submitted which responses. The assumption is that anonymous surveys will provide more candid feedback.

Evidence shows that the assumption is sound. If you want honest employee feedback, employees need to be confident that their responses will really be anonymous. As a rule, employees will provide feedback enthusiastically. You must be clear, however, that their responses are not tied to their performance evaluations. Some surveys emphasize this point on the survey itself. Without this disclaimer, employees will be less than candid in their responses. Whatever your policy, be sure to state it clearly on your surveys.

Anonymous or confidential surveys are trickier to implement than surveys you can track, and for that reason a high level of participation is harder to assure. Some employees may conclude that if they can't be tracked, there's no way for you to know if they completed the survey or not.

With identified surveys, you can track responses. It's simple to send follow-up e-mails to employees who have not submitted a completed survey. For anonymous surveys, this individual communication is problematic. Many firms solve this conundrum by engaging an outside survey firm to administer the survey. Company leadership assures employees that it will receive only aggregate results. "Anonymity is absolutely critical," emphasizes Core Practice's Frehse. "It's why we as an outside party hold the survey responses. We give the analyzed results to management, but we never give them the completed surveys. Those remain our property. It's the best way we've found to convince employees that it's safe to say what they really think."

Many employees will still hesitate to answer tough questions honestly. If you promise confidentiality, you must avoid using unique codes or URLs on the survey invitation to track the completed survey. Employees will rightly assume you defaulted on the promise.

So how do you decide? In an organization with a high level of trust between management and employees, identified surveys are easier to implement and generally do the job. Anonymous surveys are called for when the climate of trust is lacking and has to be rebuilt. Another case for an anonymous survey is when management really needs the most candid and authentic responses possible.

Asking for Demographic Information

Many surveys include a component that asks for categorizing demographic information such as gender, age, tenure with the company, department, work site, name of supervisor, job title or level, education completed, and the like. Chapter 18 includes sample demographic questions for your consideration.

Keep in mind that every piece of demographic information you collect can be used to narrow the field of the possible identity of the respondent. If you ask for gender, work location, title, and department, and you have only one female supervisor in operations at your Illinois plant, you've blown any pretense of anonymity—and that respondent will know it. Core Practice surveys never ask for demographic information that would narrow the field of possible respondents to fewer than five people.

Before you include demographic questions, think about the analysis you want to conduct, and ask only the demographic questions needed to conduct that analysis. Most large organizations find it helpful to compare survey results across divisions or departments in order to learn how different local management groups or varying business conditions are impacting employee morale. An organization wrestling with a heritage of diversity issues may want to slice data by gender to see how programs have influenced feelings of men and women.

Likewise, don't ask for demographic information if you're not willing to take action to address results on that level. In an anonymous survey for a food manufacturer, Frehse asked different crews of shift workers about alternative scheduling procedures. The management he was working with knew in advance that they were willing to implement changes on a group-by-group basis instead of across the board. When the results came back that pockets of the workforce liked the current schedules, the decision was made to maintain the current schedule for them. Other employees liked a proposed idea of longer but more predictable workdays, and as a result their schedules were changed.

Incentives

Incentives are designed to increase response rates. A typical approach is to announce that employees who submit complete surveys will be entered in a raffle that will reward one lucky winner with a prize such as an iPod, an extra day off, or some other consideration of value. Most survey professionals say that incentives do increase participation, but they can also backfire. The more valuable the prize, the more likely it is to skew results. The consensus is that gag or token gifts work best. For example, St. Louis–based Build-A-Bear Workshop, with 6,000 employees in 350 stores in North America and Europe, offers a piece of candy called a "Smartie." Bob Buer, director of Combearsation, Bearnefits, and Bearvelopment (seriously!), helped develop a campaign that started with a teaser ("Be a smartie, complete the Associate Experience Survey") and then follow-ups ("Be a smartie, don't forget to fill out your survey"). Both messages were graphically "delivered" by Bearemy, their mascot, who was drawn in an "all ears" listening position. Buer's advice is to keep incentives to token value.

Group incentives sometimes work better than individual incentives. A company can announce that the department or work group that has the best participation in the survey will win a prize such as a pizza party.

Online Surveys

In the past, companies have used mail surveys, telephone surveys, paper and pencil surveys, and personal interview surveys to get feedback from employees. Today, the advantages of implementing employee surveys using Web-based online tools are so substantial that they have almost totally eliminated the use of other methods. By eliminating the time and expense of printing and mailing, Web-based tools present new opportunities for quick, tactical surveys in an interconnected world. The dramatically lower costs now make surveys practical for businesses and nonprofits that could not afford them before. It is now possible to conceptualize, implement, and analyze a modestly sized employee survey without spending a cent. Beyond the cost advantages are increased options for automatic data processing and analysis and increased participation from employees who are connected 24–7 through laptops or smart phones.

The nature of Web-based survey tools has changed the way employee surveys are administered and consumed. On the administration end, Web-based surveys can be used almost in real time to aid in decision making. For example, a survey can help determine if a program or change effort is being rolled out effectively to every area of the organization. Web-based surveys can help an organization assess how employee attitudes change over days in response to emerging events or an initiative. For globalized organizations, Web-based surveys make it practical for the first time to survey all parts of the enterprise at the same time.

What to Look for in a Vendor

A whole industry has emerged to serve organizations large and small in their survey requirements. The tools are varied in scope and expense, but all are accessible via a browser interface from any computer connected to the Internet. The tools are designed to be intuitive and easy to use, even for nontechnical professionals. Most vendors allow users to try their offerings at no cost. They also offer a variety of free videos, white papers, and sample surveys. Of course, they hope that you will find their tools and services so compelling that you will engage them to assist you with your ongoing survey requirements.

Comparing survey software vendors can be a time-consuming undertaking. Finding a vendor that tailors exactly to your needs can be even harder. We believe you'll want to research at least three elements in order to make an informed decision as to which online survey provider is the best for you. Those elements are (1) the survey software feature set, (2) the pricing structure and model, and (3) the support you will receive once you have made your purchase.

Software Feature Set

There are literally thousands of software tools and vendors available to assist you. Many of the tools are free. A good way to start the product selection process is to consider the budget you have and the outcomes you want. Making such a list will give you a clearer idea if your requirements include:

- Guaranteeing anonymity
- Automated survey features such as scheduling e-mail survey invitations and resending the survey to nonresponders within a designated time frame
- Manual entry of paper survey results for employees who may not have Internet or e-mail access
- Availability of survey forms on handheld mobile devices

- Distributing reports by e-mail
- Flexibility in survey layout and formatting

Pricing Structure

Each survey vendor has its own unique pricing structure, and it's important to know exactly how each one works. So when comparing survey companies, be sure to understand the terms of the contract, find out if there are discounts associated with a longer contract, and make sure you know what is included and not included for the price you are paying.

Customer Support

The third part of your survey provider comparison is to determine what type of customer support you expect as well as what type of customer support the company provides.

Selecting a Vendor

The following Web directories can help you quickly locate many reputable vendors:

- HRmarketer.com: Vendor profile section allows you to search through hundreds of HR software vendors, including survey vendors, for many options: http://www.hrmarketer.com/ community/, then enter "surveys" as keyword in Vendor Quick Search box.
- Capterra.com: Capterra's online software vendor directory can help you locate many potential vendors covering many different software categories (so you can use it to find more than just feedback software). Their free RFP (request for proposal) service allows you to send your requirements to a variety of vendors and have the vendors contact you.

- HR.com: Using a buyer's guide broken down into many categories, you can find vendors by "communities" of common interests.
- SHRM.org: Using the buyer's guide, go straight to the survey categories for survey software vendors.

The good news is that vendors make it easy for you to try their products. So go ahead. Make up a short test employee survey of 20 questions or so. Also make up a small distribution list of about 20 e-mail addresses of your colleagues. Make sure your own e-mail address is on the distribution list. Now implement the test survey by using a number of the tools provided by the software. Make a note of how intuitive the software is. When you execute the test survey, make a note of how quickly it's delivered. Do the formatting and logic work? What's the experience of the recipients as they complete the survey? How clear are the reports? Based on this information, you will quickly zero in on the tool and vendor that best suits you.

None of this technology changes the fundamentals. In order to get an effective employee survey, you still need a valid design supported by reliable survey items that are relevant to the organization and reflect its goals and culture.

This book assumes that the survey you create will be administered mostly by electronic means. Remember that some of your employees may not have access to a computer or be comfortable using a mouse and keyboard. For those employees, and for those with certain disabilities, be sure to provide the survey in a format they can use easily.

Even though the ease of online surveys is unmatched, you may want to include some face-to-face components. As noted earlier, presurvey conversations or focus groups can help alert you to issues as you design and write a survey. Some organizations like to add depth to quantitative data by interviewing a select number of random (or, in some cases, hand-picked) respondents in person as well. Be careful to treat input from those limited interviews as the limited view they necessarily represent.

Time Frame for Responses and Sending Reminders

As you plan your survey time line, include enough time for employees to complete the survey but not so much that it becomes easy to put on the back burner. Using its experience with consumer surveys, marketing communications firm Trone likes to give a two-week window for completion. If someone is travelling, ill, or on vacation, chances are that they will be back within that time frame.

Trone's Kevin Murphy says that one group of employees will answer within the first three days. Then you'll likely have a "weekend effect" during which few people will answer and the e-mail with the survey can get buried deep within an inbox. Murphy suggests that you send a reminder to everyone after about 7 to 10 days: "When you send one reminder, you get a 25 to 30 percent lift in participation. But two or three reminders can make those surveyed feel like they are being stalked."

Trone's survey process allows the company to tally the department from which the responses come. In the first reminder, Murphy makes use of the healthy competitive spirit within his company by reporting which department has the highest participation rate. "Not only do we plug into their competitive nature," says Murphy, "we also emphasize that without responses, we can't know what their department is thinking. What department wants other departments' voices to be louder?"

From the Field

Here is the text of the reminder Trone sent to employees seven days after the initial distribution of their last survey.

REMINDER: Trone 2008 Employee Survey

Surveys are due by Wednesday EOD. So if you haven't done so already, please take a few minutes to complete the 2008 Trone Employee Survey available online at: [link included].

Your feedback will be invaluable in making Trone a more rewarding place to work. As I mentioned originally, the survey is totally confidential and completely anonymous so don't hesitate to let your voice be heard! Individual surveys will not be shared with anyone. You may complete your survey on any computer with an Internet connection, so feel free to take it offsite if you're more comfortable with that. We need your survey by end of day Wednesday, [date].

As of now we have 45 percent response rate from Creative, 75 percent from Account Management, 70 percent from Admin and 65 percent from Strategy and Research, so if you want your voice to be heard and your department's voice heard, please respond by [date].

Thanks again,

[Signature]

Response Formats

As you are formulating questions, you'll also need to develop the way in which respondents will answer those questions. The most common type of response format used in multiple-choice employee surveys is the "degree-of-agreement" scale that asks respondents to select one of the following options regarding their view of the statement in question:

1—I strongly disagree
2—I disagree
3—I somewhat disagree
4—I somewhat agree
5—I agree
6—I strongly agree
NA—Not applicable/Don't know

Putting It Together

A question to go with this scale would be formulated as a statement such as: "I am satisfied with opportunities for collaboration." Another common response format is the degree of satisfaction scale that runs from "I'm extremely dissatisfied" to "I am extremely satisfied" (see the next Perfect Phrases box). To probe the same subject, you would pose the question, "How satisfied are you with opportunities for collaboration?"

Most practitioners advise not including a neutral ground (e.g., "no opinion"), as it offers an easy out to respondents who have an opinion but may be reluctant to offer it. Another hint in the use of the degree-of-agreement response format is to keep the answer to which you aspire on the high end of the scale; for example, use the statement "there is adequate parking" rather than "there is not enough parking." Most surveys are well served if higher numbers are correlated to positive outcomes. It becomes confusing if low numbers are desirable for some questions and high numbers for other questions.

Other ideas for response formats are included in the next Perfect Phrases box. Surveys will be easier to design and complete if you limit the number of different response formats you use. Each time you change formats, the respondent needs to take time to read instructions and become acquainted with the new approach. If you are using several different formats, avoid switching back and forth between them. Instead, consolidate questions that use the same format.

For demographics and questions about options, use drop-down boxes where possible so that analysis is easier. For instance, if you want to know which benefit is most important to employees, create a drop-down box that corresponds exactly with your benefit program. That way, you won't have to handle combining write-in answers "medical insurance" and "health coverage," for example. Of course, for open-ended questions such as "What one change could we make to serve customers better?" you'll want to provide nothing but a blank page or field.

Perfect Phrases for Response Formats

In addition to the degree-of-agreement scale, Trone suggests other response formats you might find useful:

- Degree of satisfaction scale
  - I'm extremely dissatisfied
  - I'm dissatisfied
  - I'm more dissatisfied than satisfied
  - I'm more satisfied than dissatisfied
  - I'm satisfied
  - I'm extremely satisfied
- Rankings of options given: Which of the following items/ideas is ...
  - Most important, second most important, etc.
  - Least likely to succeed, may succeed, most likely to succeed, etc.
- Correlation scales: How related is one item to another (e.g., "How is the comfort of your work station related to your job satisfaction?")
  - 1—Not at all related
  - 2—
  - 3—
  - 4—
  - 5—
  - 6—Entirely related
  - Not applicable
- Rating advocacy (e.g., "How likely are you to recommend Trone as a great place to work?")
  - 0—Not likely at all
  - 1—
  - 2—
  - 3—

- 4—
- 5—Neutral
- 6—
- 7—
- 8—
- 9—
- 10—Extremely likely

Note that the rating advocacy scale is attributed to the Net Promoter® market research technique.

The Questions Asked Really Do Matter

The way the questions or statements are phrased determines the effectiveness of the survey. It's not easy to frame a question or statement so that the questions yield honest information. Experience shows that in their desire to be cooperative, survey respondents frequently slant their responses in ways that deviate from their true attitudes. They may do so because they believe that honest responses will be punished. Or, out of a sense of cooperation, they may attempt to respond as they believe their managers would want. So it is vital that the questions and statements be clear, focused on one item at a time, unambiguous, not open to interpretation, and free of unaware biases or word choices that would make the items unreliable.

The box that follows lists some of most common ways in which questions and statements are compromised.

The best way to ensure survey questions and statements are free of such defects is to test them using a group of employees who will not be part of the survey. Employees are the best candidates for these tests because they are most familiar with the subject pool and can best identify items that may be problematic.

Part Two includes hundreds of questions and statements that meet the standards for reliability.

From the Field

Ten Common Mistakes

These 10 common mistakes of survey design are provided courtesy of Diane Asyre, principal of Asyre Communications, LLC, a St. Louis, Missouri–based consultancy specializing in employee communications.

1. Don't Combine Questions

Faulty: How much do you value and use the tuition reimbursement benefit?

Solution: Separate into two items.

Perfect: How much do you value the tuition reimbursement benefit? How often have you used the benefit in the last 12 months?

2. Avoid Overlapping Ranges

Faulty: Indicate length of employment: 1–5 years [ ] 5–10 years [ ] 10 –15 years [ ]

Solution: Make sure the scales allow only one correct response.

Perfect: Indicate length of employment: 1–5 years [ ] 6–10 years [ ] 11–15 years [ ]

3. Don't Ask Leading Questions

Leading questions are items that are worded to draw a desirable response. You won't gather candid information, and your question might be interpreted as corporate window dressing.

Faulty: Our company's environmental protection plan is directly tied to job security, and we have met our goals in this area faster than expected. Agree or disagree?

Problem: In this instance, who would want to disagree? If job security seems connected to a positive response, then few employees would disagree with the statement no matter how they actually felt about the premise.

Solution: Don't accidentally use a survey item to stack the deck on either side of a debate.

Perfect: Our department is consistently able to meet the goals specified in our environmental protection plan. Agree or disagree?

4. Avoid Unclear Questions

Faulty: My career development prospects are improved by the CDC.

Problem: Unclear. What if the employee does not know what the CDC is?

Solution: Spell out abbreviations and acronyms.

Perfect: My career development prospects are improved by the Career Development Center (CDC).

5. Don't Assume

Faulty: Rate on a scale of one to five your agreement with this statement: My immediate supervisor explained how my performance rating was determined during my annual performance review.

Problem: What if the employee, for whatever reason, didn't have a performance review? Or what if the review was with someone other than the employee's immediate supervisor?

Solution: Add an item that lets the employee indicate if the assumption is correct. Then ask a separate question about whether the performance rating system was explained satisfactorily.

Perfect: I met with a supervisor within the past 12 months for a performance review.

Perfect: I have had my performance reviewed within the last 12 months.

6. Don't Ask About Issues You Can't Do Anything About

Example: Would you like to have a long-term-care benefit plan that helps you to pay for services such as nursing home expenses for you or immediate family members?

Problem: The only thing wrong with the question is asking it when there is no possibility that the company can provide such a benefit.

Solution: Be sure to involve the appropriate company decision makers when it comes to asking questions that may require further action or be interpreted as implied promises.

7. Don't Allow Self-Selection for Participation

Employees should never self-select to participate in an employee survey. When you allow self-selection, you'll generally find that employees with the most extreme opinions are overrepresented. Less communicative employees are guaranteed to be underrepresented. For valid and reliable results, either every employee should be surveyed or a random selection method should be used to decide who will be included.

8. Avoid Overly Broad Open-Ended Questions

Faulty: Tell us something that we can do to improve the company.

Problem: This overly broad question will elicit impossible responses, such as this: "Serve beer in the employee cafeteria."

Solution:	Make the question personal, and link it to an actionable outcome.
Perfect:	If you could make just one thing happen to improve product quality, what would that be?

9. Don't Forget to Offer a "Not Applicable" or "I Don't Know" Option

Survey results are distorted when respondents who don't have an opinion are forced to commit to one. Moreover, it frustrates the respondents, and they tend to abandon the survey.

10. Don't Ignore Employees Who Are Absent

The survey design should accommodate employees who are absent (on vacation, sick, etc.) during the time the survey is administered.

Part Two

Perfect Phrases

This section categorizes hundreds of survey items for you to pick from as you put together the employee survey that's right for your organization and the kind of learning and insight you're looking for. Because organizations are organic, interlinked systems, these broad categories overlap. For this reason, some survey items appear in more than one list.

Each section includes common "a la carte" items from which you can pick and choose. Many sections also include a "From the Field" box that reprints an actual survey used by an organization or developed by a survey expert. These entries are like "prix fixe" or set menus that you can adapt in their entirety.

Start by looking at the employee satisfaction and engagement surveys in Chapter 6, as they are in many ways summary surveys encapsulating the concepts in all of the other surveys. Then look at other chapters that correspond to your areas of particular interest. Where you see a blank to be filled in, insert the name of your organization or, if you are surveying on a more limited scale, the name of your business unit, division, department, or site, if applicable.

Because survey respondents are now very used to the degree-of-agreement scale, all survey items are constructed for use with that scale (on the next page) unless otherwise noted. Most experts suggest that you not offer a neutral choice but instead include a "not applicable/don't know" option.

1. I strongly disagree
2. I disagree
3. I somewhat disagree
4. I somewhat agree
5. I agree
6. I strongly agree
7. Not applicable/I don't know

Chapter 17 gives you some items for alternative survey techniques: using a mixture of positive and negative terms, using open-ended questions, and "since last year …" and degree-of-importance formats.

Take the survey items in the book as is or as inspiration for your own questions. As you make your list, be sure to replace generic terms with those that are well accepted in your organization. For instance, you might use the term "leadership team" instead of "senior management," or "associates" instead of "employees." Make sure to translate any technical terms or jargon into language that is meaningful for the employees in your survey sample.

Once you have your long list of survey items, review it for repetition and applicability, remembering to ask only about items relevant to the people you are surveying. Then compare your list to your survey goals to determine if each item will further the learning or analysis you need. Refer to Chapter 4 for a discussion about the optimum length of a survey; it's unlikely you'll want to include more than 50 items. Remember that you can always go back with a second survey probing more deeply into an area that comes up as a problem.

Chapter 5
Setting the Stage

Announcements

Announcing the Survey Process

Surveys are rarely effective if they are distributed unannounced. Employees are usually busy. Unless they get some information to the contrary, it's tempting for them to regard online surveys as just another e-mail or interruption. Ideally, the survey should be introduced in the weeks before distribution through a variety of coordinated communications vehicles, including posters, in-person announcements from supervisors, blast e-mails, and articles in the newsletter. These items remind employees why the survey is important and how the results will be used. If the survey will be confidential, reinforce that point in these communications. It's also a good idea to give the date on which the survey will be distributed and the deadline for its return.

Perfect Phrases for Announcing an Upcoming Survey

The following are sample introductory phrases with which you can open an organization-wide e-mail to announce an upcoming survey:

- The _____ survey is coming.
- Are you ready to have your opinion counted?
- Announcing the employee survey.
- Watch your inboxes for the employee survey.
- We want to hear what you have to say.
- Your opinions are important!
- Every voice counts!
- Your voice makes a difference.
- Play your role. Complete the survey.
- Results of the survey help leaders set priorities.
- Your answers will help identify priority areas for improvement.
- In the next few days/weeks, you will be invited to take part in the _____'s annual employee survey to assess employee satisfaction as well as leadership and management practices contributing to organizational performance.
- It's totally confidential. It's totally anonymous.
- As you have heard, _____ is conducting an employee survey. We/I encourage you to respond to the survey because it provides you with an important opportunity to make your opinions count.
- As we roll out our global values this year, this survey will assist us in knowing where we have opportunities to improve.

From the Field

Sample E-Mails

Example 1

In recent years, the [name of survey] has been an important tool for employee feedback. In the [date and name of last year's survey], company leaders identified four priority areas for improvement:

- Leadership practices
- Opportunities for growth and advancement
- Organizational communication
- Learning and development opportunities

Let us know how changes in those areas are working. Complete this year's employee survey to give us that feedback.

Example 2

[Name of month] signals an important process—the employee opinion survey. We place great value on this annual, anonymous survey of all employees so that we can better understand your views. This year's survey is scheduled for [dates]. Your participation is essential and greatly appreciated.

Example 3

As a central component of _____'s commitment to our people, the annual [name of survey] offers a dedicated channel for communication from our employees. Through the use of a company-wide employee engagement survey, _____ annually invites employees to contribute feedback and their perspectives through a confidential third-party-supported survey process. The project is a focused initiative through which _____ leaders apply and integrate insights gained from employee input into the daily management of their organizations and their deployment of programs and practices. On an ongoing basis, leaders monitor and communicate their activities to enhance our employee engagement objectives.

Example 4

[Name of survey] starts this week!

Help make _____ the best place to work. Take the opportunity to say how you feel about working at _____ by completing the survey. What's working? What's not? And what could be done to improve your level of job satisfaction and commitment to the organization and its goals?

The survey starts _____ and ends on _____. The survey is anonymous and completely confidential.

From the Field

Sample Introductory Letters

Example 1

(Company Letterhead)

(Date)
To all employees:

You are invited to participate in an employee opinion survey. We survey our employees every year to provide an opportunity for you to communicate your opinions about the conditions of employment at our company. The greater the participation, the more reliable the survey will be.

We will have the results of the survey within two months. At that time, an all-employee meeting will be held to review those results. That meeting will be followed by department meetings in which you can raise questions and develop suggestions for contributing to our company's work environment.

Your responses to the survey questions will be held in confidence. You will not be asked to identify yourself. The completed surveys will be collected by an outside employee opinion survey consulting firm. Its employees will be the only ones to actually see the completed surveys. They will tabulate the results and provide us with summary reports only.

As with past surveys, you will be asked to provide some personal information. Such information allows the results to be reported by different groupings of employees such as department and length of service.

If you are uncomfortable supplying that type of data, you may leave those questions blank, but I hope you will see their value and supply the requested responses. If you have any questions, please do not hesitate to contact me.

We view our annual employee opinion surveys as an opportunity to continue to improve the two-way communication process at our company.

Thank you for your participation,
(Signature and title)

Example 2

Your Survey—Your Say

Dear Colleague,

Invitation to participate in the [year] Staff Opinion Survey

I invite you to participate in an independent Staff Opinion Survey we have commissioned that will be run [dates of the survey].

When we first announced plans to run a Staff Opinion Survey, we found that staff were somewhat skeptical as to the possible benefits to be gained from such an initiative. Is it simply a PR exercise? Will it really be anonymous? Will it really help to improve working lives and quality of service?

Well, it certainly isn't a PR exercise but rather part of a commitment made to staff to improve satisfaction at work. That's why we are calling on **every member of staff** to get behind the survey and give us their views. We need to find out what you think about your working life at _____ and the areas that could be improved. The feedback we receive from the survey will be used to put together action plans to address the issues you raise. The results of the survey will be disseminated to staff by [date], and action plans will be shared by [date].

This survey is **totally anonymous**; it is being conducted in accordance with the [name of policy]. The results will be analyzed by [name of vendor], an independent consultancy. Your questionnaire will never be linked to you as an individual.

> You will receive a copy of the survey during the week commencing [date]. If you have a work e-mail address, you will receive an e-mail from [name of vendor] containing a link to the Web page from which you can access the online survey. If you do not have a work e-mail address, you will receive a paper copy of the survey.
>
> Remember, this is your opportunity to help by sharing your thoughts with us. No matter what our roles are in this organization, we all have a vested interest in the future of _____.
>
> Yours sincerely,

Announcing That the Survey Is Live

Given that almost all employees have access to e-mail, the most popular method of announcing a survey is to send e-mails that contain a link to the survey. The advantage of using e-mail is that it is quick and cost effective, and the distribution of invitations can be well targeted and controlled. If the e-mails originate from a senior manager, the probability that employees will open them and respond is increased.

Some organizations use a dedicated Web site to announce and promote surveys. E-mails direct respondents to the Web site, which has a link to the survey itself. This method is ideal for confidential surveys, as respondents will have a higher degree of confidence in the anonymity of their responses. Employees correctly believe that surveys linked to individual e-mail messages can be tracked; indeed, that is their primary attribute.

Remember to announce the deadline by which time completed surveys are to be submitted.

Perfect Phrases for Announcing That a Survey Is Live

The following are sample introductory phrases with which you can open an organization-wide e-mail to announce that the survey is live:

- Make your opinions count! Please complete this employee opinion survey to help us improve our company. Your responses will remain confidential.

- At _____ we value our employees and welcome your feedback on how to continually improve our work environment. We appreciate your taking 20 minutes to complete this confidential survey.

- Last week, I announced that we would be issuing an employee survey. Click on the link below and complete the survey by [deadline] to make your voice heard.

- As part of our continuing commitment to listening to your opinions and suggestions, we are conducting a confidential employee survey. Please follow the link below to let us know what's on your mind.

- Please complete the survey by [deadline].

Introducing and Giving Instructions about the Survey

Every employee survey starts with a short statement that identifies the survey and gives instructions about how the survey is to be completed. It's appropriate to address this statement to employees who may be hearing about the survey for the first time and have never completed a survey before. By now, you're very familiar with surveys and their conventions. Don't assume that level of knowledge from other employees. Spell things out in simple terms. Don't hesitate to repeat information included in early announcements as those messages are important and can be reiterated as employees are looking at the actual survey.

The instructions should include as many of the following elements as possible:

- Name of survey
- Purpose
- Why it is important
- Deadline
- A sincere desire to listen
- A review of how last year's survey led to tangible programs and results
- Confidentiality (if it's a confidential survey)
- Instructions for completing survey

Additionally, every scale requires the survey to provide appropriate instructions or directions. For example:

- *Please select the response that corresponds to your level of agreement with the statement.*
- *Please circle the number in the scale (1–10) that best indicates your total personal experience for each of these statements.*

Perfect Phrases for Survey Instructions

Purpose

This survey is designed to gather feedback from you regarding your work experience at _____. The results of this survey will enable us to identify what we do well as an organization as well as areas that may need improvement.

Expectations

While it will be impossible to implement all suggestions made through this survey, please be assured that senior management will hear and consider all of your ideas and appreciates your input.

Anonymity

This survey is being distributed to all employees. Your responses to the survey will be completely anonymous. Survey results will be reported only in general terms.

Instructions

Please consider each question in relation to how you view the organization in general. Then mark the circle that best represents your opinion based on the scale. Please attempt to complete all questions on this form as best as you can. Questions marked with an asterisk (*) are mandatory. Your feedback is very important and greatly appreciated.

From the Field

Trone Introduces Its Survey

This is an actual example of one company's survey instructions. Trone is a marketing communications firm that has applied its technical knowledge and commitment to learning to its own employee survey process. Note how, in the introduction to their survey, they do the following:

- Express a sincere desire to listen
- Review how last year's survey led to tangible programs and results

- Set the stage for this year's survey in language that suits their culture
- Assure confidentiality
- Give instructions for completing survey
- Set a clear deadline

Trone Employee Survey

We want to hear what you have to say.

You said you needed more training . . . we created Pi training sessions and a classroom.

You said you needed better performance feedback . . . we implemented an annual review process.

You said you needed more team building . . . we brought back Field Day.

What do you need in 2009?

As we continue to make Trone a more rewarding and fulfilling workplace, we need to know how you really feel about working here. To make this work, we really need everyone's feedback. That's right.

We're shooting for 100 percent participation.

It's totally confidential. It's completely anonymous.

So tell us the good, the bad and the ugly. Again, this survey is completely confidential and anonymous, so please be thoughtful and honest in your answers. You can complete it from any computer with internet access, so feel free to do it from home if that makes you more comfortable.

We need your survey by end of day Wednesday, December 17.

Please proceed to the next screen.

Chapter 6
Employee Satisfaction and Engagement Surveys

M ost broad-spectrum employee surveys seek to gain a top-level understanding of either employee satisfaction (how happy employees are with their jobs, work environment, and prospects) or employee engagement (how aligned employees are with the mission, vision, values, and strategy of the organization and how much energy and commitment they are willing to give the organization). Combine these two generalized surveys, as organizations often do, and you have a portrait of the employees' attitudes and opinions, and how their experience of work is adding value to the organization. These kinds of surveys are particularly useful after an organization has undergone some sort of change, such as a layoff, an acquisition, or the addition of a new department head. They also help employers isolate the root causes of persistent problems, such as low productivity or high expenses.

Subsequent chapters provide more specific survey items about areas that in one way or another are subsets of employee satisfaction or engagement.

There are three general approaches you can take to maximize the benefit from these broad-brush surveys:

1. Conduct focus groups to understand the specific areas you want to probe.
2. Determine the areas of employee satisfaction and engagement that are either most important to employees (see the first section of the following Perfect Phrases box) or most aligned with your strategy, and include more detailed survey items about those areas.
3. Administer a relatively short employee satisfaction and/or engagement survey, and then conduct a follow-up survey with more detailed questions to probe those top-line results that were most surprising, interesting, or troubling.

Perfect Phrases for Employee Satisfaction Surveys

How you define employee satisfaction will depend on the kind of organization you are, your culture and, most important, what employees like yours look for in work. Therefore, each employee satisfaction survey will be different. The sample employee satisfaction survey items that follow represent the kinds of survey items other organizations have found applicable. Note that many of these general survey items are also included in the more specific survey types in later chapters in this book. See also the Build-A-Bear Workshop's employee satisfaction survey component, which is reprinted in Chapter 17, because it uses the alternative technique of asking the same question using both positive and negative language. Chapter 17 also includes a degree-of-importance survey.

Determining Most Important Drivers of Satisfaction

Many organizations begin their employee satisfaction survey with a component that asks employees to rate or rank various aspects of their environment or experience at work in terms of how important they are to their overall satisfaction. The results help your management team set priorities for change: if an element is widely chosen as important to employees and the satisfaction with that component is low, it would become a priority for change. Conversely, if an element ranks as unimportant to employees, it would not be the most appropriate focus for management time or resources, even if the satisfaction score came in very low.

Drivers of satisfaction do change over time, but you probably do not need to include this component with every satisfaction survey. It is sufficient to include it when you launch a survey process, when there have been major changes, or once every two to three years in a stable environment.

How important are each of the following aspects of work to your overall satisfaction with your job?

1 = not important at all
2 = not very important
3 = important
4 = quite important
5 = extremely important
NA = Not applicable / I don't know

	1	2	3	4	5	NA
Leadership from senior management/ Relationship with senior management						
Relationship with my supervisor						
Relationship with my coworkers						
Relationship with customers						
Relationship with suppliers						
Overall feeling of the work environment						
Recognition for good work						
Ability to contribute to society through my work						

	1	2	3	4	5	NA
Sense of accomplishment						
Feeling challenged						
Feeling empowered						
Having only reasonable demands placed on me/Not having unreasonable demands placed on me/Low workplace stress						
Communication within the organization						
Work/life balance						
Physical work environment (workspace, furniture, lighting, etc.)						
Technology and systems						
Commute						
Parking						
Pay and benefits						
Opportunities to advance in my career						
Training and development						
Job security						
What the organization stands for						
Quality we deliver to customers/ Customer experience						
Company reputation						

General

- Overall, I am satisfied at _____.
- I like my day-to-day job.
- My work is challenging and interesting.
- I like my job. It is enjoyable.
- I like my job. It is challenging.
- I look forward to coming to work.
- I find my job personally satisfying.

- I am proud to be working at ____.
- I feel honored to work for ____.
- Overall, I think _____ is successful.
- Rate your overall satisfaction on the following scale:
  1. I'm extremely dissatisfied
  2. I'm dissatisfied
  3. I'm more dissatisfied than satisfied
  4. I'm more satisfied than dissatisfied
  5. I'm satisfied
  6. I'm extremely satisfied

Sense of Purpose

- My work gives me a feeling of personal accomplishment.
- I have a sense of worthwhile accomplishment in my work.
- I feel like I am contributing positively to society through my job.
- I am proud to be working toward the mission of _____.
- I am proud of the work I do.

Feeling Valued

- ____ makes good use of my skills and abilities.
- ____ really cares about me.
- I feel this organization treats each employee as a valued member of a team.
- I feel personally valued at _____.
- _____ values me as a person, not merely the work I do.
- I am recognized for my work.
- I am recognized for my accomplishments.
- I am recognized for promoting the values of _____.

Acting on Sense of Satisfaction

- I plan to be working at _____ a year from now.
- I feel ____ is a great place to work.

- I recommend _____ as a place to work for my friends.
- I would encourage friends and others to work at _____.
- I hope to continue to work here for another five years or more.
- I would accept my job again.
- I am glad I have built my career here at _____.

Common Sources of Stress

- My workload is reasonable.
- My responsibilities are reasonable for the amount I am paid.
- My responsibilities are reasonable for the number of hours I work.
- My work environment allows me to be highly productive.
- When I travel for work, I find the organization's policies acceptable.
- At _____, I am recognized for my accomplishments.
- I am rewarded/recognized for good work.
- _____ does enough to help me balance work and life issues.
- I am able to maintain a healthy balance between my work and my personal commitments.
- _____ has instituted practices and programs that help me take care of my personal responsibilities.
- My supervisor supports my need to balance work and family issues.
- My work-related stress is manageable.

Confidence in the Future

- I am confident in the future of this industry.
- I am confident in the future of _____.
- I feel my job is secure.
- As long as I do a good job, I will continue to have the opportunity to work for _____.
- When _____'s finances improve, I'm confident I will have some share in its financial success.

From the Field

Polaris Employee Satisfaction and Engagement Survey

A general market research company, Polaris suggests this brief, wide-ranging employee satisfaction and engagement survey to its clients.

For each of the following statements, indicate if you:

- Strongly disagree
- Disagree
- Somewhat disagree
- Somewhat agree
- Agree
- Strongly agree
- Not applicable/I don't know

1. I am aware of Company ABC's overall strategy.
2. I understand what Company ABC, is trying to achieve.
3. I feel my department gets support and teamwork from other areas within the company.
4. Overall I am very satisfied with my job at Company ABC.
5. My manager clearly defines my job responsibilities.
6. My manager/supervisor encourages high achievement by reducing the fear of failure.
7. My manager/supervisor takes responsibility for shaping the attitudes and relationships within our department.
8. My manager/supervisor clearly communicates what is expected of me.
9. My manager/supervisor provides me with continuous feedback to help me achieve.
10. My manager/supervisor demonstrates professionalism.

Perfect Phrases for Employee Engagement and Commitment Surveys

Engaged employees feel passion for their work, provide drive and innovation, and feel they actually have a part in moving the organization forward. This type of survey gauges the employees' involvement with fundamental aspects of the organization and their duties. Through such surveys, you can learn about employees' level of loyalty, dedication, and involvement. Compare the results of the engagement survey with absentee levels and quality failures, as both can be symptoms of low levels of engagement.

These surveys will necessarily be tailored to your organization because they seek to learn how well employees have understood and internalized what your organization is about and how willing they are to go the extra mile in pursuit of the goals set by your leaders.

Sense of Pride

- I am proud to work for _____.
- I am proud to be working toward the mission of _____.
- I love telling people I work for _____.
- I feel I am an important part of _____.
- _____ is a catalyst of change and innovation.
- I would recommend my organization to a friend looking for a job.

Sense of Loyalty

- I am happy to share my experiences of working at _____ with others.
- It rarely crosses my mind to leave _____ to work elsewhere.

- I walk the extra mile and exceed the expectations of my managers.
- Working at _____ gives me a feeling of achievement.
- To help _____ achieve its goals, I contribute more than my share.

Connection to Organizational Goals

- I know how my work relates to the agency's goals and priorities.
- I have a good understanding of the goals of this organization.
- I understand how my job contributes to _____'s bottom line.
- I understand how my job contributes to _____'s overall performance.
- I understand how my job contributes to the success of _____.
- In my most recent performance appraisal, I understood what I had to do to be rated at different performance levels.
- In my work unit, differences in performance are recognized in a meaningful way.
- Pay raises depend on how well employees perform their jobs.
- My performance appraisal is a fair reflection of my performance.
- My job is important within _____.
- I understand the link between my job and _____'s objectives.
- My job allows me to make full use of my knowledge, skills, and abilities.
- I understand the goals of my department.
- In my department, we talk about how we're contributing to the bigger picture of the organization.
- I can explain our business goals to others.
- I can explain our vision to others.

Empowerment and Accomplishment

- Doing my job well gives me a sense of personal satisfaction.
- My skills are effectively used on the job.
- I feel empowered to perform the work required once a task has been assigned.
- My suggestions are given serious consideration by managers.
- I am involved in key decisions that impact me at work.
- I appreciate that I am held accountable for my performance.
- _____ motivates me to perform to the best of my abilities.
- The work processes adopted by _____ allow me to be productive.
- When it comes to executing my duties, I'm entrusted with the authority to make necessary decisions.
- _____ demonstrates that it is committed to my career development by providing me with adequate training opportunities.
- The criteria for employee recognition are well established at _____.

Perfect Phrases for Surveys about Engagement with Core Concepts

Core concepts include the vision, mission, values, and strategy of the organization: the elements management articulates to set a direction and a foundation for the organization. If you want to measure employee awareness of your organization's vision or any of the other concepts in this section, you should first use an open-ended question to ascertain what, if anything, employees have absorbed and how they express it. Then, separately, you can use a multiple-choice approach to go more deeply into the thoughts and feelings about that concept. Alternatively, use the first question about awareness to get a rough, self-reported read on awareness levels.

Remember to pose survey items about one concept at a time; for instance, don't combine all the values in one statement as respondents may have different reactions to different values.

1. The vision at _____ is [vision]. Please indicate your degree-of-agreement with the following statements:

   - I was aware of this vision before reading this survey question.
   - I understand what this vision means.
   - Management has done a good job communicating this vision.
   - I understand how my job contributes to the vision.
   - I believe we can achieve this vision.
   - The way we're operating now will lead us toward achievement of this vision.

2. Our mission at _____ is [mission]. Please indicate your degree-of-agreement with the following statements:

   - I was aware of this mission before reading this survey question.
   - I understand what this mission means.
   - Management has done a good job communicating this mission.
   - I understand how my job contributes to the mission.
   - I believe in this mission.
   - This mission matches my personal values and priorities.
   - The way we're operating now lets us fulfill this mission every day.
   - Our mission is relevant to our customers.
   - Policies and procedures are aligned with this mission.

3. One of our values at _____ is [value]. Please indicate your degree-of-agreement with the following statements:
   - I was aware of this value before reading this survey question.
   - I understand what this value mean in practice.
   - Management has done a good job communicating this value.
   - Management acts in accordance with this value.
   - I understand what it means to act in accordance with this value.
   - I believe we as an organization can act in accordance with this value.
   - The way we're operating now exemplifies this value.

The following questions can be asked of all of the values put together:
   - The values listed are the ones I see at play within the organization.
   - My personal values match these values.
   - Policies and procedures are aligned with these values.

4. The essence of our strategy at _____ is [short version of strategy]. Please indicate your degree-of-agreement with the following statements:
   - I was aware of this strategy before reading this survey question.
   - I understand what this strategy means.
   - Management has done a good job communicating this strategy.
   - I understand how my job contributes to the achievement of the strategy.
   - I believe this strategy is the right path to take.
   - The way we're operating now is indeed implementing this strategy.
   - Policies and procedures are aligned with this strategy.

From the Field

Trone Employee Survey

Marketing communications firm Trone's technical knowledge regarding survey and research design, as well as their multiyear experience honing their own employee survey, has resulted in the following set of questions that we reproduce here in its entirety.

2008 Trone Employee Survey

1. What part of the organization do you work in?
2. How long have you worked at Trone?
   - Less than a year
   - 1–3 years
   - More than 3 years
3. Did you take the employee survey last year?
   - Yes
   - No
4. How satisfied are you with Trone as a place to work?
   - I'm extremely dissatisfied
   - I'm dissatisfied
   - I'm more dissatisfied than satisfied
   - I'm more satisfied than dissatisfied
   - I'm satisfied
   - I'm extremely satisfied
5. How satisfied are you with the progress we have made over the past year?
6. How satisfied are you with the direction the agency is going?
7. How likely would you be to refer a friend or colleague to work at Trone? Please respond with a "0" meaning "not likely at all" up to a "10" meaning "extremely likely."
   - 0–Not likely at all

- 1
- 2
- 3
- 4
- 5–Neutral
- 6
- 7
- 8
- 9
- 10–Extremely likely

8. To what extent is your overall satisfaction working at Trone directly related to your experience with your clients? Please indicate your answer with a "1," meaning that your overall satisfaction is not at all related to the clients you work with, up to a "6," meaning that your overall satisfaction is entirely related to the clients you work with. If you don't interact with clients, please check "not applicable."
   - 1–Not at all related
   - 2
   - 3
   - 4
   - 5
   - 6–Entirely related
   - Not applicable

9. Thinking about your experiences at Trone over the past year, please indicate your level of agreement with each of the following statements, with a "1" meaning "I strongly disagree," up to a "6" meaning "I strongly agree."
   - I know what is expected of me at work.
   - I have the materials and equipment I need to do my work right.

- I have the training I need to do my work right.
- At work, I have the opportunity to do what I do best every day.
- In the last 30 days, I have received recognition or praise for doing good work.
- My supervisor seems to care about me as a person.
- My supervisor encourages my development.

10. Thinking about your experiences at Trone over the past year, please indicate your level of agreement with each of the following statements, with a "1" meaning "I strongly disagree," up to a "6" meaning "I strongly agree."
    - At work, my opinions seem to count.
    - My role at Trone makes me feel my job is important.
    - I am confident in the leadership of executive management.
    - My associates or fellow employees are committed to doing quality work.
    - I have a good friend at work.
    - I am satisfied with the new performance review process.
    - This last year, I have had opportunities at work to learn and grow.
    - The vision for the company has been defined to my satisfaction.

11. As you think about the upcoming year, please indicate your level of agreement with each of the following statements, with a "1" meaning "I strongly disagree" up to a "6" meaning "I strongly agree."
    - I need more of a clear picture of what is expected of me.
    - I need to be better equipped (i.e., equipment, tools, books, subscriptions, etc.).
    - I need more training (i.e., PI sessions or industry training).
    - I need to be in a different role that better utilizes my talents.

- ■ I need to be recognized for my contributions more regularly.
- ■ I need to know that I am valued as a person, not just as an employee.
- ■ I need a mentor who sponsors my career growth.

12. As you think about the upcoming year, please indicate your level of agreement with each of the following statements, with a "1" meaning "I strongly disagree," up to a "6" meaning "I strongly agree."
    - ■ I need more opportunities to voice my opinions.
    - ■ I need Trone to better deliver on our vision.
    - ■ I need more leadership from executive management.
    - ■ I need to feel proud about the work I perform.
    - ■ I need more mutual trust between my co-workers.
    - ■ I need more frequent or regular feedback about my performance.
    - ■ I need more opportunities to learn and grow.
    - ■ I need the performance review process to be improved upon further.

13. As you think about the upcoming year and your needs at Trone, which of the following things is the *most* important?
    - ■ I need more of a clear picture of what is expected of me.
    - ■ I need to be better equipped (i.e., equipment, tools, books, subscriptions, etc.).
    - ■ I need more training (i.e., PI sessions or industry training).
    - ■ I need to be in a different role that better utilizes my talents.
    - ■ I need to be recognized for my contributions more regularly.
    - ■ I need to know that I am valued as a person, not just as an employee.
    - ■ I need a mentor who sponsors my career growth.
    - ■ I need more opportunities to voice my opinions.
    - ■ I need Trone to better deliver on our vision.

■ I need more leadership from executive management.

■ I need to feel proud about the work I perform.

■ I need more mutual trust between my coworkers.

■ I need more frequent or regular feedback about my performance.

■ I need more opportunities to learn and grow.

■ I need the performance review process to be improved upon further.

14. As you think about the upcoming year and your needs at Trone, which of the following things is the *second* most important? Please be sure not to select the response you gave for the last question.

15. As you think about the upcoming year and your needs at Trone, which of the following things is the *third* most important? Please be sure not to select either of the responses you gave for the last two questions.

16. What do you like *most* about Trone?

17. What makes Trone a rewarding place to work?

18. If you could change anything to make Trone a better agency, what would it would be?

19. If you could change anything to make Trone a better place to work, what would it be?

Thank you for your time. You have been very helpful!

From the Field

Laird Technologies' Employee Satisfaction Survey

Laird Technologies is a leader in the design and supply of customized products for wireless and other advanced electronics applications. It employs over 10,000 people in operations in North America, Europe, and across Asia. Laird is a subsidiary of Laird PLC, a public company headquartered in London. The survey items that follow fall into the "Caring" section of its extensive global employee survey, and use a degree-of-agreement scale.

- My work gives me a feeling of personal accomplishment.
- I feel valued as an employee of Laird.
- My work group leader acts with compassion, integrity, and honesty in all situations.
- I feel that my opinions and differences are valued.
- Even if I were offered a comparable position with similar pay and benefits at another company, I would stay at Laird.
- I would recommend Laird as a great place to work.
- I believe that employees displaced during this economic downturn have been treated with dignity and respect.
- I believe that Laird Technologies' severance benefits are fair and appropriate.

Chapter 7
Leadership and Management

E mployee satisfaction and engagement are directly related to the quality of leadership, the decisions leaders make, and the policies and procedures they design and enact. Survey items in this chapter will help you understand how your employees view both senior management and direct supervisors.

Perfect Phrases for Surveys about Leadership/Senior Management

These survey items are about the people at the very top of your organization. Some organizations use the term "leaders" or "leadership team." Others use "senior management," "the executive committee," or, in some larger organizations, "corporate management." Pick the term that is right for you. We've used a variety of terms to give a full flavor. In your statements, you'll want to be specific and use the title that is well understood by your employees and corresponds to the level of leadership you want to learn about.

Integrity

■ I trust management to do the right thing.
■ Senior management acts with compassion in all situations.

- Management "walks the talk" when it comes to values.
- Senior management acts with integrity in all situations.
- Senior management acts with honesty in all situations.
- When management tells us something, we believe it.
- Senior management discourages nepotism/favoritism at _____.

Setting Direction

- At _____, managers communicate a clear sense of direction.
- Management gives staff a clear vision of the direction in which we are going.
- Senior leaders have clearly established a direction for _____.
- Management explains why we operate the way we do.
- Senior leaders reinforce a productive corporate culture.
- Senior leaders promote a great place to work.

Mutual Respect

- Senior managers listen to me and care about my ideas.
- A member of senior management has visited my work site within the past six months.
- Senior management has demonstrated an interest in my work group's efforts.
- Senior management is connected to what we do in my division.
- Management respects me.
- Management respects how hard I work.
- Senior managers respect everyone equally, regardless of his or her level in the organization.
- When management says, "People are our most valuable asset," I believe them.
- Senior management's credibility is high.

- I have respect for the job the senior leaders are doing.
- I respect the senior leaders as people and role models.

Competence and Leading the Business

- Members of management are leaders in their fields.
- In my organization, leaders generate high levels of motivation and commitment in the workforce.
- Senior management knows what it's doing.
- Management has a good plan to assure future growth of our business.
- Management sets challenging but reasonable performance targets.
- Management sets challenging but reasonable production targets.
- Senior management has improved over the past two years.
- I have confidence in the direction management is taking the organization.

Communication

- I can talk to senior management if I have a problem or issue.
- Senior managers listen to me and care about my ideas.
- Management encourages staff to ask tough questions.
- Senior management communicates the state of our industry.
- Senior management is honest and open about the prospects for our organization and our jobs.
- My manager does a good job of sharing information.
- Senior management communicates well with the rest of the organization.

- Communication is encouraged at _____.
- Information and knowledge are shared openly within _____.

Action from Survey

- I believe action will be taken based on the results of this survey.
- I believe that action, where practical and appropriate, will be taken based on the results of this survey.
- I believe that management will take the results of this survey seriously.
- Senior management took action based on last year's survey.
- Members of senior management explained what they learned from the last survey.

Inspiration and Morale Building

- Management does a good job creating excitement about working here.
- Management builds morale among employees.
- Management helps, not frustrates, situations.
- Management does not interfere with getting the job done.
- Senior management tries to balance the organization's requirements with the interests of employees.
- Senior management does a good job balancing the needs of all stakeholders.
- Senior management does a good job balancing the need for performance with employees' needs.
- Management makes sure there are enough people to get jobs done right.

From the Field
Laird Technologies' Survey about Managers

Here's how Laird Technologies asks about managers at several levels:

- Senior management communicates a clear sense of direction for my business group.
- Senior management is effectively managing our business during these difficult economic times.
- My local management is effectively managing our business during these difficult economic times.
- I believe that I receive the right amount of information on the status of our business from the leadership team.
- I understand the strategies by which my business group will achieve its goals.
- I can see a clear link between my work and Laird's objectives.
- I have confidence in my business group's senior management to lead us to achieve our goals and objectives.
- Laird is making the changes necessary to compete effectively.

Perfect Phrases for Surveys about Supervisors

Most people who leave their jobs voluntarily say they do so because of dissatisfaction with their immediate supervisor. It's therefore very important to understand how your employees view the quality of their direct management. In addition to a broad, confidential survey, you may want to undertake a 360-degree feedback process in which each supervisor receives direct feedback, usually within a performance review setting, from three directions: their own management, their peers, and the people who report to them.

General

- My manager is a competent professional.
- My supervisor is technically confident.
- My supervisor knows what s/he is doing.
- My manager provides me with timely information on the organization's direction and growth.
- I see strong evidence of effective leadership from my supervisor.
- What one thing could your supervisor do to make your job more fulfilling? [open ended]
- What one thing could your supervisor do to make your job more satisfying? [open ended]

Setting an Example and Ethical Leadership

- My manager sets a good example for others to follow.
- My supervisor is a role model in terms of his/her quality of work.
- My supervisor is a role model in terms of his/her work ethic.
- My manager treats employees with fairness.
- My supervisor treats me fairly.
- My manager respects my thoughts and feelings.
- I am satisfied with my supervisor.
- I look up to my supervisor.
- My supervisor has good people skills.
- My manager administers policies and procedures consistently.
- My supervisor follows through on promises made.

Communications and Accessibility

- I am kept in the loop by my supervisor.
- My supervisor honestly communicates important decisions to me.

- My supervisor lets me know what is happening in the organization.
- My supervisor gets my input and buy-in when making key decisions that impact me at work.
- My supervisor involves employees in solving problems facing the department.
- My manager is open and honest.
- My manager is transparent in communicating with me.
- My manager is accessible and approachable.
- I am comfortable talking to my supervisor.
- My supervisor listens to my suggestions.
- My supervisor is available when I have questions or need help.
- If I can't solve a problem with my supervisor, I know whom to contact.

Expectations and Objectives

- I know what my supervisor expects of me in my job.
- My supervisor delegates effectively.
- My supervisor sets performance goals for my job.
- My supervisor gives me enough resources to get the work done.
- Last-minute assignments and/or schedule changes do not occur more frequently than they should.
- Work assignments are fairly distributed.
- My supervisor has enough authority to make decisions needed to keep us on track.
- My supervisor has enough authority to allocate resources within our work group.

Development

- My supervisor regularly talks with me about my progress.
- My supervisor supports my goals for self-development.

- My supervisor works with me to develop my skills and abilities.
- My supervisor spends enough time with me.
- My supervisor encourages professional development of employees.
- My supervisor works with me to identify training and development opportunities.
- My supervisor helps me organize or delegate my work so that I can attend training sessions.

Feedback and Recognition

- When I do a good job, I receive the praise and recognition I deserve.
- My manager recognizes me when I do a good job.
- My supervisor provides me with feedback concerning the job I do.
- I receive useful and constructive feedback from my manager.
- Employee performance evaluations are fair and appropriate.
- I am given adequate feedback about my performance.

From the Field

Opinions Incorporated's Survey Items about Supervisors

Opinions Incorporated is a full-service opinion research organization that produces and administers customized surveys. From their catalog of hundreds of survey items, they suggest that you select no more than 48 questions total. The following list about immediate supervisors touches on all aspects of the relationship between bosses and subordinates.

Leadership and Management

- My supervisor takes responsibility for his or her mistakes.
- There is good cooperation between supervisors and higher levels of management at [site].
- My supervisor gives me recognition when I do a good job.
- My supervisor does a good job of scheduling work and setting deadlines.
- My supervisor gives credit where credit is due to the employees.
- I am satisfied with the way my supervisor treats me when I make a mistake.
- We are encouraged to speak our minds, even if it means disagreeing with our supervisors.
- When I know that my supervisor is wrong, I don't fear punishment if I confront him or her.
- I feel my supervisor is doing a good job.
- My supervisor is very clear about the amount and quality of the work that is expected from me on my job.
- My supervisor gives prompt attention to problems on my job.
- I feel free to go to my supervisor and discuss things that bother me.
- My supervisor is available when I need to talk or meet about work-related matters.
- My supervisor makes me feel appreciated.
- My supervisor has confidence in me.
- My supervisor cares about my development needs and career progress.
- My supervisor understands my problems.
- My supervisor requires people to do high quality work.
- My supervisor is willing to listen if I want to discuss a personal problem or concern.

- My supervisor asks for people's ideas about work-related problems.
- My supervisor gives me the feedback I need to help me perform my job well.
- My supervisor explains the reasons for his or her decisions.
- My supervisor clearly explains tasks and job assignments so that employees know what is expected of them.
- My supervisor consults me when changes are being made that affect me or my work.
- My supervisor gives serious thought to what employees have to say before making a decision.
- My supervisor understands my job well enough to help me if I have problems.
- My supervisor tries to build teamwork within our group.
- Our department supervisor does a good job of coordinating the work of our group.
- My lead person is competent and does a good job.
- When necessary, it is possible to make changes in the way we do things here.
- My supervisor listens and responds to employee concerns.
- My supervisor gives me the time I need to discuss things important to me.
- My supervisor or someone at this location seems to care about me as a person.
- There is someone at this location who encourages my development.
- My immediate supervisor is a good communicator.
- My immediate supervisor has good management skills.
- My immediate supervisor is effective in directing our group to accomplish its goals.
- My immediate supervisor is a good leader.

Leadership and Management

- My immediate supervisor effectively promotes teamwork within our group.
- My immediate supervisor is committed to achieving results for our organization.
- My immediate supervisor is knowledgeable about my job functions.
- My immediate supervisor has good decision making skills.
- My immediate supervisor takes accountability for his or her actions.

Chapter 8
Values and Ethics

A primary role of leaders is to set, articulate, and behave according to the values of the organization and to set the ethical tone for the organization. Survey items in this chapter are designed to help you learn about employees' understanding of and commitment to the fundamental principles underpinning the integrity of your organization. These survey items assume that there is some clarity among the leadership team as to the values and ethical standards of the organization. If your organization has yet to develop such clarity, or if there has not been a recent discussion of values and ethics, you may want to hold off surveying employees on this topic. Instead, you'll want to involve them in exploratory discussions.

The first portion of this chapter focuses on values and ethics in general, and then subsequent sections give you survey items for specific values that are common to many organizations. Chapter 9 covers common topics in organizational culture; depending on the definitions you use, some of those topics may fall into the values category for you.

Perfect Phrases for General Surveys about Values and Ethics

Awareness and Understanding

- At _____, we operate in accordance with a high ethical standard.
- I have a clear understanding of _____'s values.
- The organization's values are: [open-ended question]
- I can explain our values to others.

Values in Action

- I see the organization's articulated values in action every day.
- Management "walks the talk" when it comes to values.
- My supervisor "walks the talk" when it comes to values.
- Senior management acts with compassion in all situations.
- Senior management acts with integrity in all situations.
- Senior management acts with honesty in all situations.
- Senior management is honest and open about the prospects for our organization and our jobs.
- Most behavior within the organization is in line with the articulated values.
- The values management talks about provide a clear guideline for employee actions.
- At _____, people generally live the values they espouse.

Personal Alignment

- My personal values are in line with _____'s values.
- I don't feel as if I have to compromise my personal values in order to be successful at _____.

- I enact the values in my everyday actions.
- _____ is a place where I can be myself.

To Customize for Your Organization

Most organizations espouse more than one value. In most cases, you will learn more by asking survey questions about the values one at a time; see Chapter 16, "Perfect Phrases for Testing the Success of Messages," for questions designed to probe awareness, understanding, and commitment to individual values. In this section, survey items address the value set as a whole for those who need a shorter, more top-line survey. If the survey results are surprising, you will want to conduct a secondary survey to look into employee views of the individual values.

Our values at _____ are [values]. Please indicate your degree-of-agreement with the following statements:

- I was aware of these values before reading this survey question.
- I understand what these values mean in practice.
- Management has done a good job communicating these values.
- Management acts in accordance with these values.
- I understand what it means to act in accordance with these values.
- I believe that we as an organization can act in accordance with these values.
- The way we're operating now exemplifies these values.
- The values listed are the ones I see at play within the organization.
- My personal values match these values.
- Policies and procedures are aligned with these values.

From the Field
Opinions Incorporated's Survey Items about Ethics

- I do not have to violate my personal principles to do my job well.
- The company's policies on ethical business conduct are clearly formulated.
- The company's policies on ethical business conduct are well communicated.
- Pressures to meet goals and deadlines do not result in unethical conduct.
- I consider all business practices at [site] to be ethical.
- _____ encourages employees to discuss a company activity that appears to be unethical.
- If an unethical practice occurred, I feel there is someone I can talk with who would address the problem.
- This organization reinforces and practices ethical business conduct.

Perfect Phrases for Surveys about Trust and Truthfulness

Surveying employees about concepts such as trust and truthfulness is complicated by the fact that different employees have different definitions of these terms. So in the directions for this section, it is often helpful to provide a definition. For example: *"Please use this definition of trust when answering the questions: 'Trust is the willingness to be vulnerable with another because they have integrity, concern for you, competence, and shared common objectives.'"*

- My department atmosphere is consistently one of trust.
- I trust my supervisor.

Values and Ethics

- I trust my coworkers.
- I trust _____ to tell employees the truth.
- Management demonstrates its commitment to building a trusting work environment.
- Telling the truth is valued at _____.
- I would be reluctant to tell my supervisor bad news for fear of being punished as the messenger.
- Employees at _____ can deliver bad news without fear of punishment.
- I can disagree with my coworkers without fear.
- I can disagree with my supervisor without fear.
- At _____, management values honest answers.
- _____ values honesty.
- When things go wrong, we focus on fixing the problem instead of blaming people.

Perfect Phrases for Surveys about Caring

- _____ cares about me.
- _____ cares about me as a person.
- _____ truly cares about the customers we serve.
- _____ cares about the impact our operations have on the environment.
- I believe _____ would do the right thing for customers, even if we lost money doing it.
- People at _____ care about each other.
- Senior management cares about employees.
- _____ cares about the long-term welfare of employees.
- Management cares about my opinions.
- At _____, we are recognized for caring about customers.

Values and Ethics

- My manager treats all his/her employees fairly.
- The organization's policies for promotion and advancement are always fair.
- Favoritism (special treatment) is not an issue in raises or promotions.
- My manager is always consistent when administering policies concerning employees.
- I am always treated fairly by my manager.
- Everybody is treated fairly in this organization.

Perfect Phrases for Surveys about Respect

- At _____, employees are not afraid to disagree with others, including management.
- The welfare of an ill or injured employee is important to management.
- My coworkers respect me as a person.
- My manager always treats me with respect.
- My manager listens to what I'm saying.
- My manager values my talents and the contribution I make.
- The organization values the contribution I make.
- This organization respects its employees.

Perfect Phrases for Surveys about Diversity

- _____ works to attract, develop, and retain people with diverse backgrounds.
- People with different ideas are valued at _____.
- My ideas and opinions count at work.

- No one is rejected for being different.
- I can voice my opinion, even if it's different from my supervisor's.
- At _____, it is clear that jokes making fun of specific groups of people are not acceptable.
- _____ provides a supportive environment for women.
- _____ provides a supportive environment for African-Americans.
- _____ provides a supportive environment for all people regardless of race.
- _____ provides a supportive environment for all people regardless of sexual orientation.
- _____ provides a supportive environment for people with disabilities.
- Diversity training is widely available.
- Diversity training is effective.
- There is open and honest communication about diversity issues.
- It is acceptable to discuss diversity issues when they occur.
- _____ works to attract, develop, and retain people with diverse backgrounds.

From the Field

CustomInsight's Survey Items about Diversity

- People who challenge the status quo are valued.
- I can disagree with my supervisor without fear of getting in trouble.
- I am comfortable sharing my opinions at work.

- We work to attract, develop, and retain people with diverse backgrounds.
- People with different ideas are valued in this organization.
- My ideas and opinions count at work.

Perfect Phrases for Surveys about Corporate Social Responsibility/Environment

Corporate social responsibility (CSR) is a term that captures all the ways a business enterprise meets or exceeds stakeholder expectations on human, social, ethical, and environmental topics. Related terms are "triple bottom line" and "sustainability." Organizations survey employees to see if the culture, programs, and day-to-day practices support overall CSR goals and claims. Asking employees about compliance, which has to do with adherence to laws and regulations, is a different kind of process for which legal issues can vary widely by industry and country. For that reason, compliance surveys are not included here.

David Youssefnia of Critical Metrics, LLC, suggests that surveys about corporate social responsibility and the environment be sent electronically so as not to use resource-rich paper, even if it's recycled. He also suggests that the incentive given for survey completion be a donation to a charity or cause (e.g., "For each survey completed, $10 will be donated to ...").

General Commitment

- At _____, there is a commitment to social responsibility.
- _____ makes a positive difference to the world.
- I believe our products/activities contribute positively to society.

- _____ does a good job balancing the needs of all stakeholders.
- At _____, published statements about corporate social responsibility communicate what really happens in the organization.
- Senior management is committed to doing the right thing.
- At _____, business dealings are open and honest.

Human Rights

- Work practices at _____ protect the dignity of all employees.
- I am confident that _____ does not use child labor anywhere in the world.
- Working conditions at _____ are appropriate for all employees, regardless of location.
- _____ pays living wages all over the world.

Health and Safety

- _____ provides adequate protection for my safety when I am at work.
- _____ cares about my health and well-being.
- All safety guidelines are followed at _____.
- Management does not ask us to go around safety procedures.

Environment

- _____ has made efforts to reduce the environmental impact of its operations.
- I am aware of what I can do at work to reduce my impact on the environment.
- _____ encourages carpooling.
- Work schedules at _____ make carpooling feasible.

- _____ encourages use of mass transit.
- Work schedules at _____ make use of mass transit feasible.
- We could reduce our use of natural resources at work by: [open-ended question]
- We could reduce our energy use at _____ by: [open-ended question]
- Management is open to hearing suggestions for reducing _____'s impact on the environment.
- The recycling program at _____ is adequate.
- The recycling program at _____ is convenient.
- We could recycle more at work by: [open-ended question]

Community Investment: Volunteerism

- Employees at _____ are encouraged to volunteer in their communities.
- Senior management role models volunteerism.
- My supervisor role models volunteerism.
- _____ supports my decision to volunteer.
- My supervisor encourages me to volunteer in the community.
- Volunteer opportunities made available to me are interesting.
- At _____, volunteering is part of the culture.
- Volunteering is well supported at _____.
- I don't feel pressure to volunteer in ways that I don't want to.
- Volunteering isn't an extra requirement on my personal time.
- I am interested in giving my time outside of working hours.
- I am interested in spending part of my paid working time volunteering.

Community Investment: Philanthropy

- _____ gives enough money/goods to worthy causes.
- I am supportive of the philanthropy decisions _____ has made.
- I am proud of the donations _____ makes.
- The philanthropy committee is open to employee opinions about where to give money/goods.
- I think we are supporting the right charities.
- I have made use of the matching gift program.
- I am supportive of the company asking for United Way donations at work.

Community Investment: Support of Local Area

- _____ is well respected in the local community.
- _____ does what it can to support the local community.
- I think that _____ contributes appropriately to the local community.
- _____ keeps as many jobs as possible in the local community.
- Management at _____ is active in the local community.

Stakeholder Engagement

- _____ listens well to outside stakeholders.
- _____ is open to learning from outside organizations.
- _____ has changed its practices because of stakeholder input.
- _____ balances the needs of all stakeholders effectively.
- I am encouraged to listen to outside stakeholders.
- I am expected to engage with outside stakeholders.

Chapter 9
Aspects of Organizational Culture

Your optimal culture will depend on your strategy, leadership, heritage, and industry. This chapter begins with general survey items and then presents specialized survey items corresponding to common themes in organizational culture.

Perfect Phrases for Surveys about Views of Organizational Culture

■ A corporate culture is sometimes defined as the general atmosphere of a company—the way shared values, ethics, beliefs, procedures, styles, and behaviors add up to give a unique feeling. Given that definition, what words come to mind to describe the corporate culture at _____? [open-ended question]

■ There is a consistent atmosphere across our organization.

■ When senior managers talk about "our culture," I understand what they mean.

■ I understand why culture is important.

- Please select the top three words from the following list that you would use to describe the environment at _____.
  [Customize this list to include cultural attributes you desire as well as items that are quite different from what you want; include 20 to 25 terms total. If possible, supply an open-ended field under the selection "Other."]

Collaborative	Familylike	Performance-oriented
Team focused	Results-driven	Focused
Competitive	Laid back	Complex
Ambitious	Easy	Academic
Ingenious	Cautious	Intellectual
Innovative	Fast-paced	Fair
Creative	Driven	Objective-oriented
Risk tolerant	Growth focused	Highly political
Risk seeking	Extravagant	Quiet
Risk averse	Cost-conscious	Robust
Friendly	Hierarchical	Other: _____
Caring		
Serious		

Perfect Phrases for Collaboration and Teamwork Surveys

Across the Organization

- All employees work hard to make _____ successful.
- Most employees go above and beyond to help make _____ successful.
- Teamwork is encouraged at _____.

Aspects of Organizational Culture

- Teamwork is practiced at _____.
- There is a strong feeling of teamwork and cooperation at _____.
- It really feels like everybody is on the same team at _____.
- People at all levels throughout _____ cooperate effectively with one another.
- At _____, we address conflicts openly.
- There is a strong spirit of teamwork and cooperation among employees.

Within Work Group

- My team cooperates to get the work done.
- In my department, we cooperate to get the work done.
- Employees in my department participate in deciding how the works gets done.
- I know what my teammates expect of me.
- My coworkers are committed to doing quality work.
- My coworkers work well together to accomplish our goals.
- My work group resolves conflict honestly, effectively, and quickly.
- My work group has a climate in which diverse perspectives are valued.
- My supervisor involves employees in solving problems facing the department.
- My colleagues give due respect to my thoughts and feelings.
- An environment of trust is fostered within my work group.
- My colleagues display a positive attitude.
- Work assignments are fairly distributed.
- Staff meetings have open and honest participation

On Behalf of Customers/The Bottom Line

- My work group has a strong focus on the customer.
- My work group focuses on solving problems instead of finding fault.
- In my work group, we ask our internal customers how we're doing.
- My work group is aware of what customers (external) require of us.
- My work group looks for ways to improve processes and productivity.

Between Department/Divisions

- My work group receives effective communication from other work groups.
- There is good teamwork between departments/divisions.
- There are formal incentives to help out other departments or divisions.
- When I ask for help from other work groups, I get it.
- Other work groups that provide services or products to us ask for our feedback.
- My work group is aware of what internal customers require of us.
- Management does a good job avoiding favoritism.

Perfect Phrases for Surveys about Risk Taking, Innovation, and Change

- _____ is open to new ideas.
- Creativity is valued at _____.
- I am encouraged to come up with new ideas.

Aspects of Organizational Culture

- When someone makes a mistake, it is not held against him or her.
- The organization is open to new ideas and initiatives.
- I believe that the organization acts on the feedback provided by employees
- There is an appropriate balance between the formal policies and the use of judgment and common sense.
- _____ handles change well.
- At _____, we embrace change.
- The pace of change at _____ is reasonable.

Perfect Phrases for Surveys about Entrepreneurial/Action-Oriented Cultures

- We focus on achieving business and customer outcomes.
- At _____, the focus is on accomplishment, not effort or "busy-ness."
- I am encouraged to feel like an owner of our company.
- I feel connected to our business as if it were my own.
- Employee ambition is a trait valued at _____.
- Employees receive appropriate recognition for their accomplishments.
- Employees are empowered to serve customers.
- Employees are encouraged to take ownership of business results.
- Occasional failures are not penalized.
- I can explain our business goals to others.
- I get charged up when I think about the prospects for our business.
- Action plans are always implemented.
- Action plans result in clear improvements.

From the Field
Laird Technologies' Survey on Entrepreneurial Spirit

As a large corporation with business units all over the world, Laird Technologies includes survey items about entrepreneurial spirit within the company.

- I am free to take informed risks in getting my work done.
- I believe that action will be taken based on the results of this survey.
- At Laird, informed risk taking is valued regardless of the outcome.
- I can be successful in my work group and still retain my individuality.
- I understand why a diverse workforce is important to Laird's success.
- I can effectively manage the amount and pace of my work.
- In my work group we focus on both "winning" and "having fun" as part of the Great Place to Work value.
- In my business group, innovation and creative thinking are actively encouraged.

Perfect Phrases for Surveys about Empowerment and Autonomy

- I am encouraged to come up with better ways of doing things.
- I am encouraged to initiate tasks or projects that I think are important.
- I am free to use my own judgment in getting the job done.
- I am given the freedom to find new and better ways to get the job done.

- Management does not interfere with getting the job done.
- I don't have to inform an unreasonable number of people about decisions I make.
- Employees are empowered to act in the best interests of the organization.
- I am encouraged to break the rules in order to serve a customer.
- I am held appropriately accountable for the work that I do.
- I have input into the decisions that affect me.
- I know and understand my job responsibilities.

From the Field

Opinions Incorporated's Survey Items about Autonomy

Opinions Incorporated's list of survey items about autonomy captures the full cycle of this topic.

- I can take action without having my supervisor/manager approve a decision.
- I am satisfied with the amount of freedom we are given to solve work-related problems, permitting me to perform my job better.
- I am satisfied with the amount of independent thought and action I can exercise in my job.
- I have the chance to participate in determining my work methods.
- I have the freedom to set some personal work objectives.
- I have enough say about how I do my job.
- I feel personal responsibility for the work I do.
- I have enough decision making freedom to perform my job effectively.

Perfect Phrases for Surveys about Balance (Work/Family and Work/Life)

- What's most important at _____ is getting the job done, not staying late every night.
- I am encouraged to balance my work responsibilities with my personal life.
- My manager respects the value of work/life balance.
- I can arrange my work schedule to meet my personal and/or family needs.
- There are seldom schedule changes or urgent requests that make it difficult for me to fulfill my family responsibilities.
- I am satisfied with my child care arrangements.
- I am satisfied with my elder care arrangements.
- _____ should do more to help me arrange better child care.
- _____ should do more to help me arrange better elder care.
- The company does enough to help me balance work and life issues.

From the Field

CustomInsight's Survey Items on Work/Life Balance

CustomInsight proposes the following survey items about work/life balance, stress, and work pace.

- The environment in this organization supports a balance between work and personal life.
- My manager understands the importance of maintaining a balance between work and personal life.

- I am able to satisfy both my job and family responsibilities.
- I am not forced to choose between job and family obligations.
- The pace of the work in this organization enables me to do a good job.
- The amount of work I am asked to do is reasonable.
- The organization has reasonable expectations of its employees.
- My job does not cause unreasonable amounts of stress in my life.

Perfect Phrases for Surveys about Openness and Communication

- _____ does a good job communicating information about changes that may affect employees.
- Information and knowledge are shared openly within this organization.
- My manager does a good job of sharing information.
- Senior management communicates well with the rest of the organization.
- Company communications are accurate.
- Company communications are timely.
- Communication is encouraged in this organization.
- Important decisions at _____ are honestly communicated to the employees.
- Management works hard to listen to employees.
- There is open and direct communication within the organization.
- I believe that action will be taken based on the results of this survey.

From the Field

Opinions Incorporated's Survey Items on Communications

Opinions Incorporated's entry on communication, reprinted here, presents a range of questions from which you'll be able to pinpoint the precise communication issues you'd like to explore in your organization.

- I do not receive conflicting orders from above.
- Communication between top management and employees at the division level has improved in the past few years.
- Communication between top management and employees at _____ has improved in the past few years.
- Communication between management at _____ and top management at the division level has improved in the past few years.
- Communication from management is very good.
- I feel the results of this survey will be carefully studied and action taken where practical.
- Management keeps us informed about decisions and policies that affect us.
- My supervisor regularly communicates with me about my performance.
- We receive accurate information from management.
- Management makes a good effort to keep us informed about the conditions in our industry that affect our jobs.
- Employees are kept informed about issues that are important to them.
- When changes are made, current management does a good job of explaining the changes.

Aspects of Organizational Culture

- The feedback that I get from my supervisor and from my peers is sufficient to allow me to do a good job.
- I feel comfortable talking to members of management about my problems.
- It is easy to get an idea from my level up to higher levels at _____.
- When employees get the chance to communicate with higher levels of management, management really does listen.
- The company provides regular opportunities for the employees to communicate with higher levels of management.
- I am kept informed about the company's business performance.
- My ideas are reviewed and followed up on by management.
- Management is open and honest about things I need to know.
- Our location supports open communication between all levels.

Chapter 10
Work Environment

What may seem like small details to management often have a great impact on employees' day-to-day experiences at work. Ask them about these small details, and you're showing that you're interested in their comfort and well-being as well as efficiency.

Perfect Phrases for Surveys about the Physical Environment/Workplace

Overall Environment

- The physical environment of my workplace is appropriate for the type of work I do.
- The organization's policies and procedures support an effective work environment.
- Physical conditions (for example, noise, temperature, lighting, cleanliness) allow employees to perform their jobs well.
- Elevators/escalators work well and do not decrease my work efficiency.
- There are adequate services available to me on-site.

- Restroom facilities are adequate.
- Restroom facilities are clean and comfortable.
- There is ample parking.
- I feel safe in the parking lot.
- Parking policies are fair.
- What's missing from your work environment that could help you perform better? [open-ended question]

Cleaning and Maintenance

- Equipment is maintained satisfactorily.
- Office machines are well maintained and in good shape.
- Facilities are well maintained and clean.
- The workplace is clean and orderly.
- Management ensures that cleaning and housekeeping are done appropriately so that I can be effective in my job.

Food and Drink Service

- I am satisfied with the employee cafeteria.
- The hours of food service match my needs.
- The price of food is reasonable.
- The variety of food is satisfactory.
- I can find food options to meet my dietary needs.
- There are food options that match my tastes.
- There are adequate water fountains/access to drinking water.
- The coffee stations are satisfactory.
- I am satisfied with the break room.

Personal Work Area

- My work area is well lit.
- My work area is quiet.

- My work area is free of distractions.
- My work area is set up in such a way that I can be effective and efficient.
- My furniture is comfortable so that I can be efficient.

Safety and Security

- Employees are protected from health and safety hazards on the job.
- Security procedures are adequate to keep employees safe.
- Security procedures are adequate to keep our company's physical assets safe.
- My personal belongings are safe at work.
- I understand why we have security procedures in place.
- Security procedures do not interfere with my job performance.
- My organization has prepared employees for potential security threats.

From the Field

Opinions Incorporated's Survey Items about Safety

Opinions Incorporated's entry on safety, reprinted here, reminds us that safety is an important day-to-day responsibility that affects every employee.

- The safety rules and regulations are followed at [site].
- Management does everything possible to prevent accidents at [site].
- Safety policies and practices encourage me to perform my job in a safety conscious manner.

- I have been adequately trained in safety practices and procedures.
- My supervisor/team leader actively supports the safety program.
- Our safety program receives a high enough level of emphasis and activity.
- Safety training prepares/prepared me to be a safe worker.
- Suggestions made to improve safety in my workplace are implemented.
- Safe work practices are still followed even under conditions of increased production pressure.
- Management is committed to a safe workplace.
- Management is concerned about the safety of the employees.
- In my work environment we use safe practices and procedures.
- I am encouraged to report safety violations.
- I work in a safe place.
- Safety training is important at our location.

Perfect Phrases for Surveys about Resources and Access to Information

- I have the materials/tools/equipment to do my job well.
- I have the materials/tools/equipment to perform efficiently.
- I am able to obtain all the information I need to do my job well.
- ___ offers technology to help me serve my customers.
- I am never frustrated by the lack of materials/tools/equipment.
- I am never frustrated by broken or poor-quality tools/equipment.

- ____ provides me with the necessary resources to do my job well.
- My supervisor gives me enough resources to get the work done.
- I have been trained to use technology effectively in my work.

From the Field

CustomInsight's Survey Items about Workplace and Resources

Survey provider CustomInsight suggests in its catalog these survey items about workplace and resources.

- I have the resources I need to do my job well.
- The necessary information systems are in place and accessible for me to get my job done.
- I have all the information I need to do my job effectively.
- My workplace is well maintained.
- My workplace is a physically comfortable place to work.
- My workplace is safe.

Perfect Phrases for Surveys about Scheduling

Scheduling, particularly for shift workers and those whose hours change from week to week, can be a major source of satisfaction or stress. When schedules change at the last minute, it can be hard for employees to make or maintain plans with family or friends. And when hours are cut, workers earn less to support their families.

- My work schedule is predictable.
- I am scheduled for an adequate number of hours per week.
- I am scheduled for hours that I have said I can work.
- My supervisor takes my needs into account when scheduling me.
- I receive my hours far enough in advance to make plans.
- Schedules are available in a way that is convenient to me.
- I am not asked to work too many hours.
- It is my choice if I want to work overtime.
- I receive recognition for staying until the job is done.
- Policies regarding shift switching are reasonable.
- I have enough flexibility in my schedule to do my work and fulfill family responsibilities.

From the Field

Core Practice's Survey about Overtime

The surveys undertaken by Core Practice seek to gauge employee opinions on work scheduling and allocation change options. Yet the firm emphasizes that the survey must look at the complete dynamic of satisfaction. Multiple factors are often in play: demographics, areas for improvement, potential stumbling blocks, and satisfaction with leadership. For example, if you ask a question about how much overtime employees would like to work, you should also understand why they want to work it.

How much overtime would you like to work?
a) None
b) 2 hours per week
c) 4 hours per week
d) 6 hours per week

e) 8 hours per week
f) 10 hours or more per week

Do you depend on overtime for your lifestyle?
a) Yes
b) No

Do you see health and safety issues occurring due to employees not getting enough rest?
a) Yes, often
b) Yes, rarely
c) Never

Does your current schedule give you enough time off with your family?
a) Yes
b) No

Does your current schedule give you flexibility to meet the needs of your personal life?
a) Yes
b) No

Do you have responsibilities outside of work that impact your availability?
a) Yes, I am involved in volunteer activities (coaching, scout leader, etc.)
b) Yes, I go to school
c) Yes, I am responsible for people that require care
d) Yes, I have a second job
e) Yes, other
f) No

Have you considered leaving the company?
a) Yes, for better work

b) Yes, for better pay
c) Yes, for a better schedule
d) Yes, other
e) No

Compared to other area businesses, your current employer has
a) Excellent pay and benefits
b) Good pay and benefits
c) Okay pay and benefits
d) Low pay and benefits

The management team is dedicated to improving employee morale.
a) Yes
b) No

Perfect Phrases for Surveys about Policies and Procedures

You may want to substitute the word "rules" for policies and proce-dures within your organization.

■ For the most part, policies and procedures make sense within our organization.
■ At _____, policies and procedures are consistent.
■ Policies and procedures do not interfere with my ability to serve customers.
■ Policies and procedures at _____ have resulted in a more efficient operation.
■ Policies and procedures at _____ have resulted in increased safety.

- Policies and procedures promote cooperation.
- Policies and procedures do not stifle innovation.
- Policies and procedures promote high quality.
- Policies and procedures promote fairness within the organization.
- I have input into the policies and procedures that affect me.
- Management listens to employees when developing policies and procedures.
- Policies and procedures are well communicated and easily accessible to employees.
- Changes in policies and procedures are well communicated.
- Policies and procedures are updated as needed.
- Policies and procedures are aligned with the values the organization talks about.

Perfect Phrases for Surveys about Working with Suppliers

Compliance laws and industry standards have led to a number of procedures surrounding interactions with suppliers. For those employees who deal with suppliers, those rules as well as the organization's approach to procurement relationships can affect satisfaction. Here are a few survey items to ask those employees about their experiences.

- At _____, purchasing protocols are fair.
- At _____, purchasing decisions are made based on objective inputs.
- At _____, all significant purchases are put out to a competitive bid.

- I am not required to buy from certain suppliers who have personal relationships with others in the organization.
- I have received training concerning the limits on gifts I may accept from suppliers.
- I understand the rules regarding gifts from suppliers.
- Rules regarding gifts from suppliers are fair.
- Rules regarding gifts from suppliers are clear.
- _____ helps me share our policies with suppliers I work with.
- I am proud to represent _____ to our suppliers.
- I am satisfied with the way _____ treats suppliers.
- If I have a problem with a supplier, I have the authority to address the issue directly.

Chapter 11
Business Performance

Your employees are the company's representatives to customers, stewards of your quality, and creators of your value. It's important to know what they understand and believe about your organization's performance. They have a vested interest in your success and a good handle on what's working and what's not. Often, the answer to issues you face or the next big opportunity is inside an employee's head. Use a survey to tease out that information.

Perfect Phrases for Surveys about the State of the Business

Long-Term Prospects

- Our industry is growing.
- Our long-term prospects are strong.
- I am confident in our organization's prospects for the future.
- _____ is well placed to grow over the coming years.
- Management has a good strategy to keep _____ successful.
- Management has a good plan to assure future growth of our business.

Current Performance

■ I am satisfied with my work group's performance.

■ Our business performance is better than last year.

■ Our productivity is better than last year.

■ Our product quality has improved since last year.

■ Our service delivery has improved since last year.

■ We're serving our customers better than we did last year.

■ We're meeting our customers' needs better than we did last year.

■ We're negotiating better terms with our suppliers than last year.

■ Management has a good plan to pull our company out of this rough patch.

Reputation

■ Our reputation has improved since last year.

■ Customers know us as a high-quality company.

■ We are well respected in our industry.

■ We have a strong reputation with [stakeholder: customers/suppliers/regulators/within the industry/in the community, etc.]

■ The reputation of _____ matches what we really are.

Competitive Advantage

■ Compared to our competitors, _____ is [attribute desired].

■ I know what makes _____ different from our competitors.

■ I know what makes _____ better than our competitors.

Personal Connection to Business

- I can explain our business strategy to others in the company.
- I feel connected to our business as if it were my own.
- I get charged up when I think about the prospects for our business.
- Even though times are tough now, I have confidence we will make it through.

Perfect Phrases for Surveys about the Customer Experience

No one knows customers' needs like those who are in direct contact with them, so many companies survey their employees' opinions on quality and customer care. A well-designed quality or customer care survey can help organizations improve areas where service may be lacking or quality may be decreasing and lead to plans to increase customer satisfaction. Field salespeople who often work independently and remotely have special insight that can be hard to bring into the organization. A survey is a great way to gather that insight. Keep in mind that their work environment and styles are quite different from those of your in-house teams, and adapt your survey design and administration accordingly.

Commitment to Customers

- Our company is committed to providing competitive products and services to its customers.
- The organization demonstrates that delivering customer value is its highest priority.

- To better serve our customers, _____ is committed to excellence in all activities.
- Management ensures that delivering customer value consistently is made a high priority.
- Decisions made demonstrate that customers are a top priority.
- My department has a strong focus on the customer.

Insight into Customers

- I understand what issues our customers face.
- I understand what customers need.
- My department is aware of what customers require of us.
- I believe _____ does enough to understand what customers really need.
- When I share insights about customers, management listens.
- I am encouraged to share insights about customers.
- _____ acts on knowledge about customer needs.

Meeting Customer Needs

- I am able to meet my customers' needs.
- I keep promises I have made to customers.
- _____ supports my ability to deliver a high standard of quality to my customers.
- The organization is flexible about modifying company standards in order to serve customers.
- In the past six months, I have violated a company rule in order to serve a valued customer.
- People I work with are committed to exceeding internal or external customer expectations.
- The customers I come in contact with treat me with respect.

From the Field

Opinions Incorporated's Survey Items about Customer Experience

The following survey items about customer expectations are from Opinions Incorporated.

- My supervisor and I agree on the customers' expectations.
- I know my customers' expectations.
- I am measured by how well I meet my customers' expectations.
- _____ understands the expectations of our customers.
- My work activity is driven by customers' expectations, not local management direction.
- Pressure to meet budgets and schedules does *not* take priority over meeting customer expectations.
- _____ delivers products and services that meet customers' expectations.

Perfect Phrases for Surveys about Quality and Continuous Improvement

Quality

- Compared with competitors in our industry, the quality of the products made at _____ is better.
- At _____, quality is as important as cost control.
- I understand the quality expectations of my job.
- I have the authority to stop production when the quality of our product is in question.
- I have management's support on quality issues I might see as I do my job.

- My location does not violate quality standards in order to meet revenue/production expectations.
- Management's decisions and actions support the organization's quality policies.
- I have the materials and equipment I need to do my job.
- I know what is expected of me to maintain the company's quality standard.
- My fellow employees are committed to quality work.

Continuous Improvement

- Leadership encourages us to focus on how to improve quality and service.
- _____ strives to get better every day.
- The continuous improvement program at _____ is effective in promoting quality.
- The continuous improvement program at _____ is relevant.
- The continuous improvement program at _____ drives results.
- I am encouraged to come up with new and better ways to do things.
- I am rewarded for improving processes/increasing productivity.
- I am encouraged to eliminate noncritical tasks and processes.
- I am recognized for eliminating noncritical tasks and processes.

From the Field

CustomInsight's Survey Items about Customer Focus

The following survey items about customer focus are from CustomInsight.

- People are held accountable for the quality of work they produce.
- The quality of our products and services is very important to this organization.
- In this organization we maintain very high standards of quality.
- This organization understands its customers' needs.
- This organization is extremely focused on its customers' needs.
- Customer needs are the top priority in this organization.

From the Field

Build-A-Bear Workshop's Guest Experience Survey

Build-A-Bear Workshop is a company with 300 stores in North America employing a variety of full- and part-time people to deliver a high-quality customer (or, in their terms, "guest") experience in which customers "build" a customized stuffed animal. This excerpt from its 94-question survey seeks to gauge employees' views of the quality of the guest experience.

For the following statements, please rate how well Build-A-Bear Workshop delivers high quality guest experiences:

	Excellent	Very Good	Adequate	Fair	Poor
The overall job knowledge and skills of associates to deliver high quality guest experiences.	5	4	3	2	1

The measurement and tracking of the quality of guest experiences	5	4	3	2	1
The recognition and rewards associates receive for delivering WOW guest experiences.	5	4	3	2	1
The overall quality of guest experiences provided by Build-A-Bear Workshop associates.	5	4	3	2	1
The leadership shown by the chief workshop manager in supporting your delivery of high quality guest experiences.	5	4	3	2	1
The overall effectiveness of communication to associates about providing high quality guest experiences.	5	4	3	2	1
The training provided to associates to deliver high quality guest experiences.	5	4	3	2	1

Perfect Phrases to Gain Business Insight from Employees

In order to learn about employees' ideas for the business, use open-ended questions that allow them to share whatever ideas they have. To see if your organizational culture encourages sharing of ideas on a day-to-day basis, use the survey items listed under the Entrepreneurial–Action Orientation and Openness/Communications sections in Chapter 9.

Business Performance

- Describe the essence of _____'s success.
- In what ways is _____ better than or different from competitors?
- Where do you see competitors gaining on us?
- Does the way others think about our organization match the way we talk about our organization?
- What one great idea do you have for ...
  - a product/service?
  - adding value to your job, your department, or the total organization?
  - improving the workplace?
  - making your job easier?
  - increasing productivity?
  - saving money?
  - improving management?
- What is the one thing we could do to improve the customer experience?
- How could we improve processes to be more efficient?
- How could we improve processes to make work more rewarding for employees?
- How could we improve processes to deliver better quality?
- How could we improve processes to improve products?
- How could we improve processes to save money?
- How could we improve processes to improve the customer experience?
- What changes to the organization do you think would make us more successful?
- How could management be more effective?
- How could we better reach our customers?
- How could we better market our products?
- What ideas do you have for advertising and promotion?
- What events should we sponsor to build our image among our customers?

- What ideas do you have for overcoming the [challenges you face]?
- What opportunities are out there that we haven't seized?
- What do we need to do to take advantage of opportunities?

Chapter 12
Performance, Career
Development, and Training

Knowing how you're doing and where you're going in your career—and knowing that your organization supports your growth—is a key component of employee satisfaction. Most organizations have systems for setting objectives, measuring performance, and addressing areas for development, through either new assignments or training. This chapter presents survey items you can use to see what employees think of these systems and the prospects for advancement within your organization.

Perfect Phrases for Surveys about Objectives and Performance Reviews

Objective Setting

- My supervisor sets challenging performance goals for me.
- I know what my main objectives are.
- I participate in setting my goals and priorities.
- I understand the link between my job and _____'s objectives.

- I think my job performance has improved since last year.
- Managers review and evaluate my team's progress toward meeting its goals and objectives.

Measurement of Objectives

- I understand how my objectives are evaluated.
- I understand the measures used to evaluate my objectives.
- The measures used to evaluate my performance are relevant.
- There is an objective measure for each of my objectives.
- I believe my entire contribution to the organization is evaluated by the measurements used in my performance review.

Performance Reviews

- Performance reviews are handled well.
- Performance reviews are objective and constructive.
- Supervisors don't use performance reviews to cut people down.
- Criticism is always done in a private setting.
- Criticism is always handled with sensitivity.
- In the last [time frame per your organization's standards], someone has talked to me about my progress.

From the Field

CustomInsight's Survey Items about Feedback

Feedback is an important part of formal performance reviews as well as of effective day-to-day relationships within the workplace. This list of survey items about feedback is from CustomInsight.

- I receive useful and constructive feedback from my manager.
- I am given adequate feedback about my performance.
- I receive feedback that helps me improve my performance.
- I have an opportunity to participate in the goal setting process.
- Employee performance evaluations are fair and appropriate.
- My supervisor gives me praise and recognition when I do a good job.
- When I do a good job, I receive the praise and recognition I deserve.

Perfect Phrases for Surveys about Career Paths and Promotions

- People generally advance here as fast here as they do at other companies
- _____ offers adequate career paths in my job.
- I have opportunities for advancement.
- Available jobs are posted internally first.
- I am aware of opportunities for advancement that are in other departments or at other sites/divisions.
- At ___, promotions are fair and equitable.
- I believe that career advancement is directly related to job performance.
- I feel I am prepared for bigger and better opportunities within the organization

- I've grown professionally since last year.
- I know what skills/qualifications I will need to develop in order to progress within the organization.
- I have a mentor.
- I have a mentor who is helping my professional development.
- Someone other than my supervisor is available to help me plan my career.
- I perceive that relocation would be necessary for me to progress.
- I am prepared to relocate for my job.

From the Field

CustomInsight's Survey Items about Opportunities for Growth

CustomInsight proposes these survey items about opportunities for growth.

- I have adequate opportunities for professional growth in this organization.
- I receive the training I need to do my job well.
- My manager is actively interested in my professional development and advancement.
- My manager encourages and supports my development.
- I am encouraged to learn from my mistakes.
- My work is challenging.
- My work is stimulating.
- My work is rewarding.
- I have a mentor at work.

Perfect Phrases for Surveys about Training and Development

Support for Training

- At _____, I am encouraged to seek new certifications or learning.
- At _____, we are encouraged to develop new and broader capabilities.
- All employees, not just certain levels or functions, are encouraged to pursue training opportunities at _____.
- My work area is adequately staffed so that each of us can participate in training opportunities.
- My supervisor encourages professional development of employees.
- I am satisfied with tuition reimbursement programs at _____.
- I have taken advantage of tuition reimbursement programs.
- At _____, education is valued.

Availability of Training

- _____ offers me the necessary training to do my job well.
- _____ offers real opportunities to improve my skills.
- I am aware of the available training and development opportunities at _____.
- At _____, I have opportunities to improve my job skills.
- I receive the training and support I need to do my job well.
- I feel there is sufficient cross-training to allow me to perform another job function if I have to step in.
- The training offered by _____ meets my needs.

Participation in Training

- In the past 12 months, I have participated in a training course.
- In the past 12 months, I have been given an assignment designed to teach me new skills.
- I have been cross-trained so that I can do more than one job effectively.
- My orientation program gave me enough information to perform well quickly.

Role of Supervisor

- My supervisor regularly talks with me about my progress.
- My supervisor supports my goals for self-development.
- My supervisor works with me to develop my skills and abilities.
- My supervisor works with me to identify training and development opportunities.
- My supervisor helps me organize or delegate my work so that I can attend training sessions.

Perfect Phrases for Surveys about Personal Learning and Growth

- I am satisfied with my opportunities to learn and grow.
- My supervisor demonstrates a personal commitment to my continuous learning and development.
- My supervisor is adept at developing a positive learning environment at work.
- My supervisor processes timely feedback that allows me to improve my skills.
- My manager is available to answer my questions.

From the Field

Build-A-Bear Workshop's Personal Development Survey

Build-A-Bear Workshop includes this section in its employee survey. The company demonstrates its desire to provide a work experience that gives its employees, many of whom are young hourly workers, more than a paycheck.

- I have learned how to communicate effectively with others.
- I have improved my listening skills.
- I have been encouraged to look for creative ways to perform my job.
- I have become more sensitive to others' feelings and attitudes.
- I have gained new skills.
- I have expanded the way I think about things.
- Who has contributed most to your learning? [List of manager titles provided in drop-down menu.]

Chapter 13
Recognition, Reward, Compensation, and Benefits

Employees give their employer time and energy; the employer gives them recognition, rewards, compensation, and benefits. How employees view the balance of this equation has a significant bearing on their level of satisfaction. For many employees, compensation is the linchpin of satisfaction. For others, recognition is more important. See what they think of your culture, policies, and programs by using some of the following survey items.

Perfect Phrases for Recognition and Reward Surveys

- Employees are recognized for jobs well done at _____.
- Within the past [time], I have been recognized for doing a good job.
- The kind of recognition I get is relevant to me.
- I am happy with the level of recognition I receive for my contributions to my team/department.
- I like the way that my supervisor handles recognition.
- I am motivated by the kind of recognition I receive.

- People at _____ encourage each other and recognize each other's accomplishments.
- To me, the most important forms of recognition are [select three]:
    - My supervisor telling me I'm doing a good job as I am doing it.
    - My supervisor telling me I did a good job.
    - My supervisor sending me an e-mail saying I did a good job.
    - My supervisor writing me a note recognizing my work.
    - My supervisor sending a note to my home address recognizing my work.
    - My boss's boss recognizing my work.
    - My boss's boss stopping by to tell me I did a good job/thank me for my work.
    - Customers recognizing my efforts.
    - Coworkers recognizing my efforts.
    - Being recognized in front of my colleagues.
    - Receiving a meaningful nonmonetary gift.
    - Being recognized in a company publication.
    - Being recognized on a bulletin board or in signage.
    - Winning an award.
    - Being given an extra day off in recognition of my hard work.
    - Being given a bonus related to a job well done.
- I'm rewarded for doing a good job.
- Rewards for doing a good job are relevant to me.
- I am motivated by the kinds of nonmoney rewards available at _____.
- It is clear to me what I have to do to earn rewards.
- There are awards for performance that motivate me.
- There are awards for tenure that motivate me to stay.

Perfect Phrases for Compensation Surveys

- I am satisfied with my pay and benefits package.
- I receive fair compensation for the work I do.
- Compensation at _____ is proportional to the contributions that I make.
- I'm paid fairly for what I do.
- I am paid fairly in comparison with my colleagues.
- I receive fair pay for my job compared to people doing similar work at other companies.
- My salary is competitive.
- I participate in deciding the metrics on which I will be evaluated.
- I understand how changes in the organization's compensation structure are determined.
- I understand how my pay is determined
- I understand the organization's pay policies.
- When the organization's finances improve, I'm confident I will have some share in its financial success.

Incentive Programs

- I understand the incentive programs available to me.
- The process of making general compensation decisions is transparent.
- There is transparency in how incentive payments are calculated.
- Incentive programs are fair.
- Incentive programs are implemented fairly and according to policy.
- The incentive program motivates me to achieve or exceed my goals.

Perfect Phrases for Benefits Surveys

Satisfaction with Benefits

To determine the overall sense of satisfaction with benefit plans, use the following survey items:

- I feel _____'s benefit plans meet my needs.
- I feel the benefits offered by _____ meet my needs and those of my family.
- The benefit plan is fair.
- The benefit plan is flexible enough to meet my individual needs.
- I feel satisfied with my pay and benefits.
- I feel satisfied with increases in my pay and benefits.
- I feel satisfied with the sick leave policy at _____.
- I think it's fair that employees contribute to the costs of their employee benefits.

Satisfaction and Importance of Benefits

Note that in addition to satisfaction with overall benefit plans, it may be useful to look at satisfaction on a more detailed level. It's important to understand how employees rate both the *importance of* and *satisfaction with* the different benefits you offer so that you can allocate benefit resources most effectively. For instance, if employees are very satisfied with the free dry cleaning but it is unimportant to them because they wear business casual clothes, you would know not to put more money or attention into that program.

For this survey, include only those benefits you currently offer the employees being surveyed. If you offer different benefits to different employee groups, customize surveys for each group and monitor the administration of the surveys carefully. If you ask about the importance of or satisfaction with a benefit not currently offered, you're creating the expectation that you will offer it. See the third part of this box for a survey about potential benefits.

Set this survey up so that for each benefit listed, respondents rate both the importance of the benefit and, in a separate field, their satisfaction with the benefit. Provide both of the following scales:

- Please rate the IMPORTANCE of each of the benefits to you using the following scale:
    - 1—Not at all important to me
    - 2—Not very important to me
    - 3—Somewhat important to me
    - 4—Extremely important to me
    - NA—Not applicable/don't know
- Additionally, please rate your SATISFACTION with each of the benefits to you using the following scale:
    - 1—I'm extremely dissatisfied with this benefit
    - 2—I'm dissatisfied
    - 3—I'm more dissatisfied than satisfied
    - 4—I'm more satisfied than dissatisfied
    - 5—I'm satisfied
    - 6—I'm extremely satisfied
    - NA—Not applicable/don't know

Flex time	Paid jury service
Comp time	Paid military leave
Paid vacation	Unpaid family leave
Paid holidays	Unpaid personal leave
Paid sick leave	Medical insurance
Paid family/medical leave	Wellness programs
Paid personal leave	On-site fitness center
Paid bereavement leave	Off-site fitness center subsidy

Vision care	On-site concierge services
Prescription drug coverage	Subsidized cafeteria
Dental insurance	High-end/specialized cafeteria
Health savings account (FSA, HSA, HRA)	Company-supported information technology at
Commuter reimbursement	home
Subsidized commuting	Company-provided computer
Shared van service	at home
Short-term disability insurance	Company-provided cell phone
Long-term disability insurance	Continuing education
Life insurance	Tuition reimbursement for self
Job-related travel accident insurance	Tuition reimbursement for family members
Adoption assistance	Employee assistance programs
On-site child care	Retirement plan
Off-site child care subsidy	Employer contribution to
On-site elder care	retirement plan
Off-site elder care subsidy	Matching gift program

Adding Benefit Plans

If you are considering adding new benefits, first do some legwork to understand how much the new program could cost, how it would be implemented, and how it would fit in with your organization. Make sure management is on board with adding a benefit before you ask employees what they think.

Ask employees the following questions about potential benefits:

■ Please rate the IMPORTANCE of each of the possible new benefits to you using the following scale:
   ■ 1—Not at all important to me
   ■ 2—Not very important to me

- 3—Somewhat important to me
- 4—Extremely important to me
- NA—Not applicable/don't know
- For each of the possible new benefits, please indicate your willingness to share the cost:
  - 1—Not willing to share the cost
  - 2—Willing to share a small portion of the cost
  - 3—Willing to share cost evenly with employer
  - 4—Willing to pay most of the cost
  - 5—Willing to pay for all of the benefit at market rate, if the employer organizes/provides it.

Chapter 14
The Human Resources Department

In addition to implementing the recognition, reward, compensation, and benefit programs covered in Chapter 13, the human resources department often has a wider and more important role in the organization. See how employees perceive the performance of this department by using some of the following survey items. Note that you can use similar survey items for other departments serving internal customers.

Perfect Phrases for Surveys about Level of Service Provided by Human Resources

General

- I feel satisfied with the service of the HR department.
- The HR department answers questions quickly.
- I believe the HR department is impartial.
- I believe the HR department treats my questions/complaints in confidence.

- The HR program provided by _____ allows me flexibility to meet my work obligations.

Openness and Communication

- The organization's HR department is approachable.
- HR representatives are available on my schedule.
- My HR representative is a good listener.
- I believe the HR department listens to my suggestions.
- The HR department is well informed.
- Members of the HR department can answer my questions about benefits.
- Members of the HR department can answer my questions about company policies.
- The HR department does a good job of communicating company policy.

Promotions and Staffing

- At _____, promotions are fair and equitable
- Career moves at _____ are handled fairly.
- Promotions in my work unit are based on merit.
- My work unit is able to recruit people with the right skills.
- HR helps my supervisor take steps to deal with a poor performer who cannot or will not improve.

Advocacy

- I believe the HR department is a good partner in my relationships with management.
- The HR department is a strong advocate for me.
- I believe that the HR department represents my interests well.
- I believe that the HR department understands the issues I face.
- I know I can go to the HR department for help.

Perfect Phrases for Surveys about Job Descriptions and Organizational Effectiveness

Job Descriptions

- I am familiar with my job description.
- The work I actually do corresponds to my job description.
- My job description is reasonable for the number of hours I am expected to work.
- My job description is reasonable for the money I make.
- The level of responsibility I have corresponds with my job description.
- My supervisor uses my job description to set my objectives.
- My supervisor assigns tasks that fit within my job description.
- I think my job description is a valuable tool for clarifying my job responsibilities.
- My job description has evolved as I have evolved within my job.

Organizational Structure and Assignment of Responsibility

- Lines of responsibility are clear.
- We know who is responsible for what tasks.
- We know who is responsible for each part of our organization.
- I know who needs to be informed of most situations that come up.
- I don't have to inform an unreasonable number of people about decisions I make.
- Organizational structures are clear.
- Organizational structures are well communicated.

- My department is well organized to complete the work we have to do.
- _____ is well organized to meet our customers' needs.
- _____ is organized in an efficient way.

Surveys of New Employees

The first 30 days of an employee's experience is vital to creating a relationship that is successful over the long term. For that reason, organizations are vitally interested in ensuring that the "onboarding" of new employees is effective. Many organizations send 30-day (or 60-day) surveys to all new employees to discern how the first days on the job are going. These organizations routinely survey employees at the first anniversary of their employment as well.

From the Field

New Hire Survey from Financial Services Firm

The following new hire employee survey was developed by the finance department of a large insurance company. The survey asked new hires to respond to statements by checking either "yes" or "no" or by indicating their level of agreement with each statement using a four point scale (strongly agree, somewhat agree, somewhat disagree, strongly disagree). The survey ended with open-ended questions.

Instructions: We appreciate your feedback on this brief survey to help us understand what we're doing well and what we need to improve regarding the interview process, new hire introduction, new hire training, and job-specific satisfaction. The survey will take you 10 to 15 minutes to complete. Your candid answers will be kept completely confidential.

The Human Resources Department

- My interviews were on time. (Y or N)
- My interviewer was prepared for my interview. (Y or N)
- The hiring manager kept me well informed at different points during the process. (Y or N)
- The hiring manager was available to answer my questions. (Y or N)
- Someone was available to escort me to my work area and give me a tour of the office. (Y or N)
- I had an escort to the welcome lunch for new employees. (Y or N)
- My computer and workstation was set up and ready to use. (Y or N)
- I was given timely training on all necessary software. (Y or N)
- I was given timely training on all procedures and processes applicable to my job. (Y or N)
- My e-mail address was set up and ready to use. (Y or N)
- My telephone was set up and ready to use. (Y or N)
- I was shown where I could request work supplies. (Y or N)
- My benefits were clearly explained to me. (Y or N)
- I was clear on what was expected of me the first 30 days on the job. (Y or N)
- I am aware of what I still need to learn to succeed at my job. (Y or N)
- I was given enough time to get up to speed on my responsibilities. (Y or N)
- I understand what is expected of me before I reach my three-month performance evaluation. (Y or N)
- My job matches up with the job description that I received during the interview process. (Y or N)
- I believe that by 60 days I will have obtained all the skills and knowledge needed to succeed at my job. (Y or N)

- I am satisfied with how my colleagues made me feel welcome. (Y or N)
- My manager is approachable. (Y or N)
- My colleagues are helpful in getting me up to speed. (Y or N)
- I understand the goals and mission of my department. (Y or N)
- I understand how my job contributes to the success of the organization. (Y or N)
- I believe my work is meaningful and respected. (Y or N)
- The company works hard to create a good work environment for employees. (Y or N)
- Please tell us about your first day at work. [open ended]
- Is there anything we could do to improve the interview process? [open ended]

Perfect Phrases for Exit Surveys

An exit interview is a meeting between a representative of the organization (typically someone from the human resources department) and a departing employee. Human resources departments conduct exit interviews and surveys to gather data for improving working conditions and retaining employees. The departing employee usually has voluntarily resigned as opposed to getting laid off or fired. The HR representative might ask the employee questions while taking notes or ask the employee to complete a questionnaire or online survey. Here are examples of the types of exit survey questions that employers commonly ask departing employees in one of those formats.

- What is your primary reason for leaving?
- Did anything specifically trigger your decision to leave?

The Human Resources Department

- Did your job duties turn out to be as you expected?
- What was most satisfying about your job?
- What was least satisfying about your job?
- What would you change about your job?
- Did you receive adequate support to do your job?
- Did you receive enough training to do your job effectively?
- Did _____ help you to fulfill your career goals?
- Did you receive sufficient feedback about your performance between merit reviews?
- Were you satisfied with _____'s merit review process?
- Do you have any tips to help us find your replacement?
- What would you improve to make our workplace better?
- Were you happy with your pay, benefits, and other incentives?
- How would you describe the quality of the supervision you received?
- What could your immediate supervisor do to improve his or her management style?
- Based on your experience with us, what do you think it takes to succeed at _____?
- Did any policies or procedures (or any other obstacles) make your job more difficult?
- Would you consider working again for _____ in the future?
- Would you recommend working for _____ to your family and friends?
- How do you generally feel about _____?
- What did you like most about _____?
- What did you like least about _____?
- What does your new employer offer that _____ does not?
- Could _____ have done anything to encourage you to stay?
- Before deciding to leave, did you investigate a transfer within _____?
- We welcome any other comments.

From the Field

Laird Technologies' Exit Survey

The following exit interview script is used by Laird Technologies and can be used as a survey form as well.

Employee name and ID (optional): _____

Location (country and state): _____

Business unit: _____

Role: _____

Band: _____

Manager name (optional): _____

Department: _____

Note: The exit interviews are done at the request of HR in [name of business unit]. Reports will be generated from the data gathered from these interviews. Please rest assured that no name or ID will be included in the reports. [Name of business unit] uses these reports to track employment trends across the company and within the business units, but not for individual work sites.

1. ***What circumstances led to your decision to leave your position?***

   ☐ Challenging work   ☐ Fair treatment

   ☐ Performance feedback   ☐ Relocation

   ☐ Company direction/operations ☐ Job instability

   ☐ Retirement   ☐ Rewards and recognition

   ☐ Growth and advancement   ☐ Team/coworkers

   ☐ Work/life balance   ☐ Miscellaneous/others

2. ***Are you currently employed?***

   ☐ Yes   ☐ No

3. What resources helped you locate your current position?

☐ Newspaper ☐ Internet ☐ Job fair

☐ Recruiting firm ☐ Employee referral

4. What advantages does this new position have over your former position?

☐ Challenging work ☐ Fair treatment

☐ Performance feedback ☐ Relocation

☐ Company direction/operations ☐ Job stability

☐ Retirement ☐ Rewards and recognition

☐ Growth and advancement ☐ Team/co-workers

☐ Work/life balance ☐ Miscellaneous/others

5. I understood my department's objectives.

☐ Strongly agree ☐ Agree ☐ Neither

☐ Disagree ☐ Strongly disagree

Comments: _____

6. My manager practiced open communications. (Manager is person to whom you directly report, most recent.)

☐ Strongly agree ☐ Agree ☐ Neither

☐ Disagree ☐ Strongly disagree

Comments: _____

7. Communication within my business unit was effective. (Business unit is ____)

☐ Strongly agree ☐ Agree ☐ Neither

☐ Disagree ☐ Strongly disagree

Comments: _____

8. My work was challenging.

☐ Strongly agree ☐ Agree ☐ Neither

☐ Disagree ☐ Strongly disagree

Comments: _____

9. The volume of my work was appropriate.

☐ Strongly agree ☐ Agree ☐ Neither
☐ Disagree ☐ Strongly disagree

Comments: _____

10. My job utilized my skills and abilities.

☐ Strongly agree ☐ Agree ☐ Neither
☐ Disagree ☐ Strongly disagree

Comments: _____

11. There was opportunity to develop and enhance my skills (through job assignments, experience, etc.).

☐ Strongly agree ☐ Agree ☐ Neither
☐ Disagree ☐ Strongly disagree

Comments: _____

12. There was opportunity for training.

☐ Strongly agree ☐ Agree ☐ Neither
☐ Disagree ☐ Strongly disagree

Comments: _____

13. People at [name of business unit] are treated the same, regardless of race, ethnicity, religious affiliation, sexual orientation, disability, age, gender, background, or other elements of diversity.

☐ Strongly agree ☐ Agree ☐ Neither
☐ Disagree ☐ Strongly disagree

Comments: _____

14. I experienced fair and equal treatment.

☐ Strongly agree ☐ Agree ☐ Neither
☐ Disagree ☐ Strongly disagree

Comments: _____

15. I felt encouraged to come up with new and better ways of doing things.

☐ Strongly agree ☐ Agree ☐ Neither
☐ Disagree ☐ Strongly disagree

Comments: _____

16. My manager administered [name of business unit] **policies and procedures consistently.**

☐ Strongly agree ☐ Agree ☐ Neither
☐ Disagree ☐ Strongly disagree

Comments: _____

17. My individual performance evaluation was valuable.
(Valuable = led to raise/promotion, insightful, resolved disagreement, skill development.)

☐ Strongly agree ☐ Agree ☐ Neither
☐ Disagree ☐ Strongly disagree

Comments: _____

18. The physical working environment enabled me to do my job effectively (e.g., office building, climate, work stations, safety issues).

☐ Strongly agree ☐ Agree ☐ Neither
☐ Disagree ☐ Strongly disagree

Comments: _____

19. I had the necessary tools and resources to perform my work effectively (e.g., computer, training, technical assistance, testing equipment, adequate staff).

☐ Strongly agree ☐ Agree ☐ Neither
☐ Disagree ☐ Strongly disagree

Comments: _____

20. *The morale in my work group was positive.* (Work group is peers/team.)

☐ Strongly agree ☐ Agree ☐ Neither
☐ Disagree ☐ Strongly disagree
Comments: _____

21. *Various forms of informal recognition were practiced in my work group* (e.g., acknowledge success, special days, thank-you board, non-monetary rewards).

☐ Strongly agree ☐ Agree ☐ Neither
☐ Disagree ☐ Strongly disagree
Comments: _____

22. *My base compensation/salary was competitive.*

☐ Strongly agree ☐ Agree ☐ Neither
☐ Disagree ☐ Strongly disagree
Comments: _____

23. *The* [name of business unit] *benefits program met my requirements* (e.g., life/health/dental/disability insurances, pension and retirement funds).

☐ Strongly agree ☐ Agree ☐ Neither
☐ Disagree ☐ Strongly disagree
Comments: _____

24. *My manager supported flexible working arrangements.*

☐ Strongly agree ☐ Agree ☐ Neither
☐ Disagree ☐ Strongly disagree
Comments: _____

25. *My travel requirements were acceptable* (e.g., job-related travel, not commute to work)

☐ Strongly agree ☐ Agree ☐ Neither
☐ Disagree ☐ Strongly disagree
Comments: _____

The Human Resources Department

---

26. At *[name of business unit],* **we focus on owning and achieving key business and client outcomes, never confusing effort with accomplishment.**

☐ Strongly Agree ☐ Agree ☐ Neither
☐ Disagree ☐ Strongly Disagree
Comments: _____

27. **What did you like most about your position and/or the company?**

☐ Challenging work	☐ Fair treatment
☐ Performance feedback	☐ Relocation
☐ Company direction/operations	☐ Job stability
☐ Retirement	☐ Rewards and recognition
☐ Growth and advancement	☐ Team/coworkers
☐ Work/life balance	☐ Miscellaneous
☐ Nothing	☐ No comment

28. **What did you like least about your position and/or the company?**

☐ Challenging work	☐ Fair treatment
☐ Performance feedback	☐ Relocation
☐ Company direction/operations	☐ Job instability
☐ Retirement	☐ Rewards and recognition
☐ Growth and advancement	☐ Team/coworkers
☐ Work/life balance	☐ Miscellaneous
☐ Nothing	☐ No comment

29. **What could** *[name of business unit]* **have done to retain you?**

☐ Challenging work	☐ Fair treatment
☐ Performance feedback	☐ Relocation

☐ Company direction/operations	☐ Job stability
☐ Retirement	☐ Rewards and recognition
☐ Growth and advancement	☐ Team/coworkers
☐ Work/life balance	☐ Miscellaneous
☐ Nothing	☐ No comment

30. Would you consider future employment with [name of business unit]?

☐ Yes   ☐ No

Comments: _____

Thank you for your time and input!

Chapter 15
Information Technology

For employees who use computers at work—and that is almost everybody in one way or another these days—technology and related services can have a big influence not only on productivity but also on employee satisfaction. Perhaps because of their data-driven heritage and the ever-increasing demand for their services, IT departments were among the first to institute internal surveys to gauge satisfaction with their performance. Such surveys are even more prevalent and relevant today.

These survey items use the term "IT" to stand for "information technology." Use whatever term your organization applies to the department that supports employee computers, networks, smart phones, etc.

Perfect Phrases for Information Technology Surveys

Level of Service

- I am satisfied with the service of the IT department.
- I believe the IT department delivers equal service to all employees.

- I know I can go to the IT department for help.
- The IT department answers questions quickly.
- The IT department is available when I need it.
- The IT department doesn't make unreasonable requests of my time.
- The IT department is well informed.
- I have contacted the help desk in the past six months.
- I was very satisfied with the service the help desk provided.
- Members of the IT department can answer my questions about technology policies.
- Deskside assistance is available when I need it.
- Deskside assistance is productive.

Collaboration

- I believe the IT department listens to my suggestions.
- The IT department asks my opinion about our technology needs.
- I believe the IT department treats my questions with respect.
- The IT department is a strong advocate for my technology needs.
- The IT department proposes new technology that can make me more productive.
- When I need a special technology project undertaken, the IT department is eager to help.
- When I need a special technology project undertaken, the IT department provides expert advice.

Communication

- The IT department does a good job communicating technology policy.

- The IT department does a good job communicating changes in technology.
- The IT department does a good job communicating about using technology to its full potential.
- The IT department does a good job communicating about viruses and other security issues.

Training

- The IT department does a good job communicating about training opportunities.
- Training programs run by the IT department are relevant to my needs.
- Training programs run by the IT department are convenient.
- Training programs run by the IT department are effective.
- I learn a lot when I attend an IT training session.
- Online training modules are effective.

From the Field
Volac's IT Survey

Volac's IT department uses this survey to measure its service levels as part of the key performance indicators (KPIs) associated with its business management system.

Please take the time to fill out this anonymous form on how IT can improve the service we provide. Please use a sliding scale in which **1 = very poor, 2 = poor, 3 = OK, 4 = good, 5 = very good**.

- How do you rate IT's response time to any problems you have with software and hardware?

1	2	3	4	5

- How do you rate IT's fix time for any problems you have with software and hardware?

    1   2   3   4   5

- How do you rate IT's ability to explain the problem and solution?

    1   2   3   4   5

- How do you feel about the notice period you receive of any planned downtime to systems?

    1   2   3   4   5

- How well do you feel the hardware and software provided meets your needs to do your job?

    1   2   3   4   5

- Do you have enough training to use the IT systems adequately?

    1   2   3   4   5

- How well does IT provide support that accommodates your working hours?

    1   2   3   4   5

- What one thing, if changed, would increase your satisfaction with the IT department?
  [open ended]
- Any other comments? [open ended]

Chapter 16
Internal Communications

I f employees don't know what the organization stands for—its vision and mission, its strategy to achieve those aspirations, its values and its progress—it becomes very hard for them to be fully engaged in the organization's growth and success. Part of engendering engagement is developing a culture of openness (see Chapter 9). Another part is a commitment to regular, effective internal communication through vehicles such as newsletters, Web sites, and meetings. To see how effective you are with such communications, use some of the survey items that follow.

Perfect Phrases for Surveys about Internal Communications

■ I am satisfied with the accuracy of the information I receive from the company.

■ I am satisfied with the timeliness of the information I receive from the organization.

■ ___ does a good job communicating information about changes that may affect employees.

■ Company communications convey a consistent message.

■ I understand the communications I receive from management.

- Company communications are accurate.
- Company communications are timely.
- I trust the information conveyed by the organization.
- I receive too little/just enough/too much information from the company. (Circle/select one.)
- I receive too little/just enough/too much information about company plans. (Circle/select one.)
- I receive too little/just enough/too much information about our values. (Circle/select one.)
- I receive too little/just enough/too much information about impending changes. (Circle/select one.)
- I receive too little/just enough/too much information about the state of our business. (Circle/select one.)
- I receive too little/just enough/too much information about what others in the organization are doing. (Circle/select one.)
- I receive too little/just enough/too much information about our products/services. (Circle/select one.)
- Please rate company communications on a scale of 1 to 10, with 1 being "extremely poor" and 10 being "exceptionally good."

Choice of Communications Vehicles

- I learn most about what's going on at _____ through: [drop-down box or list]
    - Informal conversations with senior management
    - Informal conversations with other employees
    - The grapevine
    - E-mail
    - Newsletters

Internal Communications

- Printed letters/memos
- Bulletin boards/posters
- Video conferences
- Internet Web site
- Intranet site
- Videos
- Audio programs (on CD or podcast)
- In person from my supervisor
- In team or department working groups
- In person in large groups from senior management
- Other [open ended]

- I prefer to receive communications through: [drop-down box or list]
  - Informal conversations with senior management
  - Informal conversations with other employees
  - The grapevine
  - E-mail
  - Newsletters
  - Printed letters/memos
  - Bulletin boards/posters
  - Video conferences
  - Internet Web site
  - Intranet site
  - Videos
  - Audio programs (on CD or podcast)
  - In person from my supervisor
  - In team or department working groups
  - In person in large groups from senior management
  - Other [open ended]

Perfect Phrases for Testing the Success of Messages

Thoughtful internal communications define the messages that need to be communicated to certain audiences. Sometimes, especially in change management and culture development programs, messages can be multifaceted, innovative (in that they introduce a concept that challenges the status quo), or otherwise challenging. Communicators often want or need evidence that employees are internalizing messages they hear and see. An employee survey is a great way to gather such quantitative evidence.

Survey items are sorted according to the internalization stage, but you will not want to use the stage headings.

Awareness of Messages

The best way to gauge awareness of a concise concept or data point is to use an open-ended survey item such as:

- Our vision at _____ is: [open ended]
- Our values at _____ are: [open ended]
- At _____, our mission is: [open ended]
- To reduce waste, we are now recycling the following items: [open ended]
- Last year, we merged with [open-ended field]. The name of our combined organization is [open-ended field].
- The company recently introduced four major product lines. Can you name them? [open ended]

When open-ended questions are not feasible or practical, a sense of awareness can be gauged using a multiple-choice technique. Provide at least twice as many selection options as accurate responses. For example, if you are testing employee awareness about the introduction of four new products, the survey question should have at least eight choices for product names, four accurate and four distracters.

- Which of the four values below are included on our "Values in Action" posters?
- From the list below, select the four _____ values.
- Which of the following are business units at _____?
- Which of the following awards did _____ win last year?
- Which of the following are recently introduced major product lines? (Please select four.)

A third option is a degree-of-agreement response option. For these items, name the message, value, product, and so on, and ask employees to indicate their degree of agreement with the statement that they are familiar with the concepts. Take care that each item references only one message.

- I've heard of [message you've communicated].
- I am aware of [message you've communicated].
- I remember when I heard about/read about [message you've communicated].
- I know that _____ has established hand sanitation stations by every restroom.
- I am aware that we are now recycling mixed paper.
- I am aware of _____'s water conservation policies.
- I am aware that we introduced [product line name] this year.
- I know that we acquired [acquired company name].
- I am aware that the new name of our company is _____.

Understanding of Messages

After employees are aware of messages, they can move toward understanding of the concepts. Multiple-choice degree-of-agreement survey items work well to gauge level of understanding.

- I understand what [message] means to the organization.
- I understand what [message] means to my job.
- I understand what these values mean in practice.
- I understand what it means to act in accordance with these values.
- I understand why we merged with _____.
- I can explain to others why we merged with _____.
- I can explain our business goals to others.
- I can explain our values to others.
- I could identify behavior/actions that indicate [message] in action.
- I understand why _____ is working to conserve water.
- I understand why _____ installed hand sanitation stations.
- An example of [message] is _____. [open ended]
- The reason we are now recycling mixed paper is _____. [open ended]

Commitment to Messages

Survey items about commitment to messages are best distributed in a broader survey that includes topics other than communications.

- I believe we can achieve this vision.
- I have changed the way I do things because I know about [message].
- I have encouraged others to change the way they do things because I know about [message].

Internal Communications

- I have done what I can to change policies and procedures that are inconsistent with [message].
- I recycle all or most of the mixed paper waste I create.
- I have used the hand sanitation station.
- I have [other desired action].
- I have used the new company name when I talk about where I work.

Chapter 17
Alternative Survey Approaches

Most of the survey items presented in this part of the book use the easy-to-analyze degree-of-agreement scale and positive language so that the desired response is a 6 ("strongly agree"). However, there are some alternative approaches that you might want to use within your survey. Four of these methods are explored here: open-ended questions, a mixture of positive and negative survey items, a "since last year" format, and a degree-of-importance survey that asks employees what they think about change options on the table. You can adapt most of the survey items in this book to one of these methods.

Open-Ended Questions

The variety of answers you'll receive from open-ended questions is both a blessing and a curse. Employees often feel they are more able to express their thoughts in open-ended questions; you'll find a richness, depth, and emotion that's impossible to see in responses to multiple-choice questions. However, open-ended responses can be hard to categorize and analyze, and not all employees are able to express themselves comfortably in a written response. When open-ended questions are left to the end of a survey, respondents may find themselves out of steam or time. When they are put at the beginning, subsequent multiple-choice questions can then feel redundant. We suggest you intersperse open-ended questions among the multiple-choice questions.

Another survey design hint: provide an amount of space (or number of allowed characters for an online form) corresponding to the length of answer you expect.

Perfect Phrases for Open-Ended Questions

- What do you like most about your job?
- What do you like most about _____?
- What do you like least about your job?
- What do you like least about _____?
- What is least satisfying about your work?
- What is most frustrating about your work?
- What's one thing that would help you be more successful at your job?
- What one thing would make your job easier?
- What one thing could your supervisor do to make your job more fulfilling?
- What one thing could your supervisor do to make your job more satisfying?
- What's missing from your work environment that could help you perform better?
- Describe your working relationship with your peers.
- The most important commitment I make at work is:
- The most important subjects raised in this survey are:
- In what ways is _____ better or different from competitors?

- If you could say one thing to the CEO/MD/president with absolutely no fear of being reprimanded or fired, what would it be?
- If you were to give some advice to a new employee regarding how to be successful at _____, what would it be?
- What is the primary reason you stay at _____?
- What else is on your mind that you'd like to share?
- Use the space below to give examples or expand on answers given to the multiple-choice questions above. Where you want to discuss a specific question, please include the question number.

The following open-ended questions pertaining to business performance are companions to items in Chapter 11.

- Describe the essence of _____'s success.
- In what ways is _____ better or different from competitors?
- Where do you see competitors gaining on us?
- Does the perception of our company match the reputation we put forward? Why or why not?
- What one great idea do you have for ... ?
  - a product or service
  - adding value to your department or the total organization
  - improving the workplace
  - saving money
  - improving management
- What is the one thing we could do to improve the customer experience?
- What changes to the organization do you think would make us more successful?

From the Field

Mixing Positive and Negative Survey Items

The following survey items are from Build-A-Bear Workshop. Note that the company seeks to ask the same item in both positive and negative ways in order to test for consistency and correlation. You may find many of these items relevant for employee populations with high rates of turnover, especially hourly employees.

- On most days I have the physical energy to perform my job duties well.
- I am willing to really push myself to reach challenging work goals.
- I put in a great deal of effort beyond that normally expected in order to help this organization be successful.
- During the past six months, I have had thoughts of leaving my job.
- I have received the training and preparation to excel at my job.
- I am prepared to fully devote myself to performing my job duties.
- I talk up this organization to my friends as a great organization to work for.
- I would accept almost any type of job assignment in order to keep working for this organization.
- When I am at work I tend to be preoccupied with demands from my personal life.
- Constantly improving my job performance is very important to me.
- I find that my values and the organization's values are very similar.

Alternative Survey Approaches

- Most days I feel emotionally drained before I even begin working.
- I get excited thinking about new ways to do my job more effectively.
- I am enthusiastic about providing a high quality guest experience.
- I am proud to tell others that I am part of this organization.
- Doing my job well is a source of personal pride.
- I am planning to leave my job within the next six months.
- I am determined to be complete and thorough in all my job duties.
- I care about the fate of this organization.
- I am ready to put my heart and soul into my work.
- I am extremely glad that I chose to work at this organization.
- I am actively searching for another job right now.
- This organization inspires the very best in me in the way of job performance.
- The number of hours I am getting meets my expectations.
- For me, this is the best of all possible organizations for which to work.
- Overall I am highly satisfied working at Build-A-Bear Workshop.
- I am highly satisfied with the support I receive from my boss's boss (that is, your second-level supervisor).
- My current job meets the expectations I had for it when I accepted the position.
- I believe there are career opportunities for me at Build-A-Bear Workshop.

From the Field
Since Last Year

Opinions Incorporated has a section of its question catalogue entitled "Compared to Last Year." Survey items that ask employees to rate the level of change can be particularly helpful if you're trying to gauge the impact of new programs, strategies, procedures, or management. Though most of the survey items listed in this part of the book can be reframed as compared-to-last-year survey items, here are some of the more common survey items organizations use in this format.

- Since last year, business has improved.
- Since last year, customer satisfaction has improved.
- Since last year, the quality of our products and services has improved.
- Management has been doing a better job over the last year than in the past.
- I am more satisfied with my supervisor than I was last year.
- I am more productive than I was last year.
- Since last year, my job performance has improved.
- I am more confident in the prospects for _____ than I was last year.
- I am as confident about the prospects for _____ than I was last year.
- The compensation scheme is more competitive than it was last year.

Degrees of Importance

Although each employee finds work satisfaction in a slightly different mix of inputs, there are often trends by job function, gender, age, or length of service. A degree of importance survey like the one that follows can help you "grade" different sources of satisfaction and compare differences across groups, if you collect basic demographic information within the same survey.

Please indicate how important each of the following items are to you. As you respond to each question, indicate the best response using the following scale:

- Very unimportant   1
- Unimportant   2
- Important   3
- Very important   4
- Not applicable/Don't Know   NA

- How important to you is the mission of the organization?
- How important to you are the values of the organization?
- How important is the work you do to _____'s success?
- How important to you is job security?
- How important to you is it to be involved in quality customer service?
- How important to you is the fairness of the way _____ treats all employees?
- How important to you is the type of supervision you receive?

- How important to you is the way _____ deals with change?
- How important to you is the overall communication at _____?
- How important to you are employment policies at _____?
- How important to you is the consistent administration of policies?
- How important to you is the overall training and development provided at _____?
- How important to you are the opportunities to advance at _____?
- How important to you is the salary you receive?
- How important to you are the benefits you receive?
- How important to you is your total cash compensation?
- How important to you is the recognition you receive?
- How important to you are the overall operating procedures of the department in which you work?
- How important to you is the performance of senior management?
- How important to you is the quality of customer service we provide?

Chapter 18
Perfect Phrases to Conclude
a Survey

M any practitioners find the most effective closing question on a survey to be "Is there anything else you would like to mention?" After offering that concluding opportunity, bring the survey to a close by thanking employees and telling them about the next steps in the process. This chapter lays out some language for ending a survey.

Perfect Phrases for Thanking Employees

It's always appropriate to thank employees for completing a survey. First of all, it's just common courtesy. Second, showing appreciation makes it more likely that employees will cooperate when the next survey comes around.

- You have now reached the end of the survey. Thank you very much for your time.
- You're done! Thanks for your time.
- Thank you for completing this important survey.

- Thank you for your honest feedback as we strive to make _____ an even better place to work.
- We know your time is valuable. Thank you for choosing to complete this survey.
- Thank you for completing this survey. We hope that you found it convenient and efficient.
- In appreciation of your time and attention, please enjoy the [incentive description] that you can now collect at [distribution place].

Perfect Phrases for Communicating Next Steps

Remember that reporting findings back to employees is the most critical component of the survey process. As you end the survey, reiterate your commitment to do so without making any promises about specific actions you'll take. For consistency, use the same language you used in your presurvey announcements, or try one of these options:

- We will have the results of the survey within two months. At that time, an all-employee meeting will be held to review those results. That meeting will be followed by department meetings in which you can raise questions and develop suggestions for contributing to our company's conditions of employment.
- This survey is just the beginning of our process of continual improvement. Within [number] weeks, the top-line results of this survey will be available to your supervisor, who will share them with your work group for discussion.

- By [date], the results of this survey will be tabulated, and members of senior management will send an e-mail summarizing what they have learned. In that e-mail, they will announce what changes are being considered based on your feedback and how you can continue to have input into the decision process.
- The top-line results of this survey will be available on the intranet site [link] by [date], and your manager will schedule a time for your HR representative to come talk to your work group about them.
- All the feedback given about your supervisor will be combined into one report with no link to individual responses. Supervisors will receive the report as part of their next quarterly performance review. All specific identifying information will be stripped out.

From the Field
Core Practice Concludes Survey with a Promise

The surveys undertaken by Core Practice seek to gauge employee opinions on work scheduling and allocation change options. The concluding language that follows captures appreciation of employee involvement, reiterates confidentiality, and previews next steps.

Thank you for the time and effort you put into this exercise that is so critical to the organization. Remember that these surveys will remain the property of Core Practice in order to protect your confidentiality. You will have full access to the compiled results, which will be presented to you next week in a shift meeting.

Part Three

If you've used a commercial online survey package or service, your survey results will be available immediately. You'll be able to do some basic data analysis and create some tables and graphs using the tools in the software package. If you want to do more involved analysis, chances are that you or someone in your organization has the skills to help you out.

Although many survey projects end with the analysis, a successful effort will take the next steps to communicate the results and concrete actions that will or will not be undertaken based on those results. This part of the book explores effective postsurvey communications and rounds out what you need to know to put your survey process together.

Chapter 19
Communicating Results

With the survey results in hand, it's time to let both management and employees know what was learned and what actions will be taken. It's crucial that the employees be actively involved in the postsurvey phase if an organization is to attain significant improvements in employee satisfaction and engagement. As organizational development consultant Leila Bulling Towne says, "If there is a small wound before the survey and then you don't communicate right away after the survey, that wound becomes a disease."

How Fast?

What does *right away* mean? To John Frehse of Core Practice, a consultancy that surveys employees as part of a process to identify opportunities to improve shift-work scheduling, it means the week following the survey. "Employees have short attention spans for this type of activity, and keeping them engaged in the process is critical," says Frehse. "Their buy-in in many cases will determine project success."

For most surveys, you don't have to move that quickly; usually, communicating results to both management and employees within a month is fine. It is a good idea, however, to send a short note the week after the survey that closes the data collection phase and previews next steps.

That short communication can buy you some time that you might need. Andy Richardson of Volac cautions, "Don't underestimate how much time it may take to react to the data. In the meantime, don't overpromise. Set priorities based on your company's strategy. People recognize you can't do everything at once." Organizations may need months of study, sometimes by task forces including rank-and-file employees, before they can develop firm action plans for the new programs and changes suggested by the employees. In that case, you should announce that certain changes are on the way. Timelines matter. If you wait too long to get back to employees, you risk reducing, rather than increasing, employee engagement.

Perfect Phrases for Initial Report to Employees

- Your opinions are important.
- Every voice counts.
- Your voice makes a difference.
- Results of the survey help leaders set priorities.
- Your answers will help identify priority areas for improvement.
- Thank you to all the _____ employees who showed their commitment to positive change by participating in the [name of survey]. We sought to measure and evaluate the level of employee engagement at _____ to determine employee perceptions, identify best practices, plan for necessary improvements, and create a benchmark for future surveys.
- The survey was administered from [start date] through [end date]. A total of [number] employees completed the survey, representing [percentage] of the organization's overall workforce. The average response rate for our industry is [percentage], according to [source], so we can feel good about our achievement. Thanks to all who participated.

- By conducting this survey, [number] has taken an important first step in identifying employee engagement levels and establishing benchmark data to measure continued progress. Senior leaders have reviewed a summary of findings. In the coming weeks and months, through a comprehensive process, your managers will begin to address priority issues that affect employees across the organization.

- As a valued employee of _____, you already know that _____ is committed to being a force of positive change through engaged employees, communication, and leadership. Again, thank you for your time and your feedback.

- Thank you again for your participation in this year's employee survey. [Number] people completed the survey, resulting in a participation rate of [number]%. The survey team is now in the process of tabulating results for presentation to management on [date]. We expect to report back to you on the results and initial thoughts about follow-up actions by [date]. In the meantime, if you have any questions about the survey process, please contact [name and e-mail].

- Your collective voice has spoken! [Number] people completed the confidential employee survey last week, giving us a participation rate of [number]%. We're eagerly awaiting the tabulation of the results so that management can take a look and then share not just the results but also their initial reaction with you over the coming weeks. Thanks again for your participation in the survey and for your ongoing commitment to _____.

- Thank you for agreeing to participate in our department's survey. Your inputs will be very valuable to us in our efforts to improve our service to internal customers like you. It will give us an idea of which areas to improve in order to give you the best service possible. As a respondent, you may appreciate knowing the results of the survey. Please give us two weeks to send a full report. Thank you for your participation.

■ Your say is important. In the [name of survey], you told us what you wanted. We are 100% committed to taking action based on your feedback. It will take us a few weeks to make specific plans. In the meantime, thank you for your participation.

If There Are Immediately Striking Responses

■ It's only been a week, so the survey team hasn't finished going through all the data. At first glance, though, it seems that you're really enjoying the new facility. We're eager to delve into the data to learn what parts of the new work environment are contributing most to your comfort and productivity and what issues, if any, remain to be addressed about our new location.

■ Though it's too early to have considered all the data you provided in the employee survey, it's already clear that you're very concerned about the possibility of layoffs in this tough economic environment. I hear your anxiety and I'm concerned, too. Times are very tough, and I appreciate all of your work and flexibility over the last six months as we've made changes to remain competitive. I know that we will come up with even better answers because of your input and ideas, and the management team is eager to receive the full survey report to see what else you've said. In the meantime, please be assured that we have business in the pipeline. Your department/site manager can answer any questions or concerns you may have. I look forward to continuing our learning and conversation.

To Management First

Almost all organizations present findings first to management, so that executives can be prepared to answer employees' questions and add perspective when findings are presented more broadly. Be careful to keep survey information tightly controlled until senior managers are briefed. You will lose credibility if executives who haven't seen the results are blindsided by questions from employees about the survey. Amanda Trombley, CEO of Beeliner Surveys, says that "executives frequently see [surveys] as 'report cards' on how they're doing and are eager to review their results." It's understandable that they will want to see their report cards before others do.

When that report card is all A's and B's, presenting findings to management is easy. When results are more critical of the job management is perceived to be doing, it can be harder to keep your survey feedback process on track. In either case, your job will be easier if you follow the following communications tips, either in writing or in a presentation to management:

- Recall the goals of the survey
- Report the sample size and participation level
- Put the survey in context
- Focus on data and avoid editorializing
- Quote verbatim comments as examples of data points
- Present objective comparisons
- Summarize conclusions
- Remind management that a survey is about listening
- Use positive language

Further explanation of each of these tips as well as sample phrases are given in the Perfect Phrases boxes that follow. Also keep in mind that it's best to share all survey results in one meeting or document: put the good and the bad out there at the same time. Start with the good news to keep minds open, and then present areas of concern. Give managers all of the top-line results at the same time so that they can make connections and form their own conclusions alongside the survey team. But also be sure to handle individual feedback in private. If there are comments or data critical of a particular member of management, don't share that data in a management meeting. Instead, schedule a one-on-one conversation to share the feedback privately.

Perfect Phrases for Recalling the Goals of the Survey

Begin your communications by reiterating the goals and scope of the survey. Refer to Chapter 2 for tips on setting and articulating goals.

As we planned the survey several months ago, we defined our goals as:

- To listen to *all employees* in order
- To learn *about their sense of satisfaction* and
- To quantify *any differences between sites*.

Today, we meet to review that learning and determine our approach to next steps in preparation of the report back to employees.

Perfect Phrases for Reporting Sample Size and Participation Level

Remind management who they are hearing from, and add validity and context to your results.

- The survey was administered from [date] through [date].
- A total of [number] employees completed the survey out of the [number] who received the link, giving us a participation rate of [percentage].
- This result represents [percentage] of the organization's overall workforce.
- The average response rate for our industry is [percentage], according to [source], so we can feel good about our achievement/so we know we have room for improvement.
- This participation rate is high enough to consider the results representative and valid.
- Since this participation rate is fairly low, we should use these survey results as only one of many inputs into our decision-making process.
- Since this participation rate is so low, the survey team recommends that we redesign and reissue the survey after a three-month waiting period.
- Participation rates by [broad demographic division] were ...
- We can say, then, that results are indeed representative of a broad cross section of our selected sample.
- Because participation rates were so low among [demographic], the survey team recommends that we explore why those rates were so low, address whatever concerns there were, and reissue the survey as soon as is feasible.

Perfect Phrases for Putting the Survey in Context

If any major events occurred just before or during the survey process, remind management so that the snapshot the survey presents can be viewed within that context. Avoid scheduling your survey to coincide with events such as a results or merger announcement, layoffs, release of related key economic indicator, etc.—unless, of course, your goal is to take a read of the impact of such an event.

This survey was administered from [beginning date] to [ending date]. Keep in mind that the following events occurred during this same time period. [examples given below]

- Gain/loss of key customer
- Announcement of award won by organization
- Announcement of key partnership/merger agreement
- Severe weather at a certain site
- Workplace accident

This event may have skewed the results to be more/less positive.

Perfect Phrases for Focusing on Data and Avoiding Editorial Comments

Survey results should carry the voice of employees, not of the survey team. Headlining comment groups as "productive" or "ridiculous," for example, does not uphold your responsibility to employees or let management draw their own conclusions.

Reporting objective numbers will increase the credibility of your message. Data is best presented in charts, graphs, and figures. Several other resources and people within your organization can give you tips on effective data presentation. You may want to include summary comments as titles of your figures. Use exact wording of the related survey question. Some examples of appropriate language are:

- Since last year, overall employee satisfaction has increased.
- The division with the highest level of satisfaction is [division].
- Satisfaction is fairly level across all divisions.
- Satisfaction is most closely correlated with [component].
- [Percentage] of employees report high levels of respect for the job management is doing.

Perfect Phrases For Introducing a Verbatim Comment

Choose verbatim comments that exemplify quantitative data. In so doing, you are presenting both objective results and the real voice of the employee. This approach is particularly powerful to add depth to results that are surprising, extreme, or different from previous benchmarks.

Introduce a verbatim comment with language such as:

- This data point is brought to life by the following representative comment: [comment].
- As one employee put it, [comment].
- Many employees commented on this issue. Some of the words they used were: [comments].
- The power of our change management program is best expressed by a warehouse supervisor at our Texas site: [comment].
- When we read comments such as these, we realized that our communication program has yet to meet its goals: [comments].

Perfect Phrases for Presenting Objective Comparisons

Benchmark this year's data with previous years to show trends. Compare local results to corporatewide results. If industrywide data or research study results are available, compare your results to those.

- Since last year, overall employee satisfaction has increased by [percentage].
- The average for our industry is [data point], according to [source].
- Among our benchmark group, the average result on this question is [data point].
- Satisfaction at our sites in the U.S. is, on average, [number]% higher than at sites outside of the U.S.

Perfect Phrases for Summarizing Results

Prepare an executive summary or "key results" section to highlight main points, especially if your survey was wide-ranging. Here's an example of a format and the kind of language you can use:

Executive Summary to Management

Survey Timing and Response Level

The yearly employee survey was conducted from October 14–31 using a new online delivery format. The goal of the survey was to listen to all employees in order to learn about their sense of satisfaction and to quantify any differences in satisfaction between divisions.

The survey was distributed to 2,435 employees at six sites. A total of 1,874 employees completed the survey, giving a response level of 77%. This response level is the highest achieved since the survey was initiated 10 years ago. Response levels were fairly even across positions and divisions; we can therefore consider the results representative of the population as a whole.

Overall Satisfaction

Overall, satisfaction has increased marginally since last year. The percentage of employees who agree or strongly agree with the statement "Overall, I am satisfied with my job" increased from 87% to 89%, indicating that we are approaching the high achieved in years 6 and 7.

Current Year	Year 9	Year 8	Year 7	Year 6
89%	87%	84%	90%	90%

Results Compared to Last Year

Compared to last year, employees report greater satisfaction with:

- Work environments, particularly technology. This result may be attributed to the full rollout of the new supply-chain computer system.
- Company communications, particularly those delivered by direct supervisors.
- Vacation, holiday, and leave policies. Note that over the past year, these policies have been standardized across sites, bringing [recently acquired divisions] up to the standard level.

The survey indicated lower overall satisfaction than last year with:

- Access to senior management, particularly among lower-level employees and in newly acquired divisions.
- Availability of overtime hours.
- Sense of job security. Note that during the survey period [two competitors] announced a merger and that the Dow Jones Industrial Average hit a one-year low. These events may have had an effect on the employees' underlying sense of job security.

The top three drivers of employee satisfaction have not changed significantly since last year. They continue to be:

- Strong sense of teamwork and collaboration within work groups.
- Relationship with supervisor.
- Competitive compensation and benefits.

Overall Satisfaction by Division and Level

The division with the greatest overall satisfaction level is [Division B], as it has been for the last five years. The two divisions with the lowest levels of satisfaction continue to be those most recently acquired, [Divisions D and E].

Employees at the director level and above report the highest rate of satisfaction (97%), followed by those at the operator level (91%). Middle management reports the lowest level of satisfaction, at 85%.

Points for Discussion

The following report gives more detail about each of these areas as well as a summary of the verbatim comments submitted by employees.

The results of this year's survey highlight the following topics for discussion among management:

- Ways to improve communication about company prospects in the dynamic and challenging economic environment.
- How to improve the integration of newly acquired divisions.
- Understanding and reinforcing the success of the line supervisors in creating satisfaction, while also improving access to and influence of senior management within divisions.
- Considering how to address the concerns of the 11% of employees who report being unsatisfied at work.

Perfect Phrases for Reminding Management That a Survey Is about Listening

Good listeners don't jump straight to solutions. What's important at this stage is that management is hearing the voice of the employees. They do not have to feel pressured to take any particular action as long as they are willing to communicate their thought process.

- When we launched this employee survey, we did so to listen to the voice of employees. What's most important at this stage is not the precise actions we take but that we demonstrate that we hear their concerns. Let's not jump into solutions at this point, but instead let's summarize what we've heard from them. We can then formulate a process for developing the most appropriate action plans.

> ■ Through this survey, employees are telling us that they are worried about the future. What can we say to them to let them know we hear their concern?

Perfect Phrases for Using Positive Language

Management generally has a strong sense of ownership of the organizational climate. Telling them they got an "F" on their report card won't motivate them to change. You're more likely to get their productive attention by indicating, for example, that the survey identified a morale issue that, if solved, could increase productivity.

■ The survey identified an employee morale issue. If we can work together to improve morale, we have the opportunity to increase productivity and reduce turnover.

■ Employees see lots of options for improving the way we serve customers.

■ Employees are motivated by seeing you in their workplace. They would like to see you there even more.

■ Your actions have a big influence on employee attitudes.

Then to Employees

The relative timing of reports to management and to employees depends on the kind of survey you've conducted and the action planning approach you're taking. John Frehse of Core Practice times the two presentations within hours of each other. The surveys conducted by his consultancy are carefully constructed to present specific options to employees regarding potential changes in shift scheduling or work organization. Since management approved each of those options prior to the survey, says Frehse, they are each acceptable after the survey: "We plan the presentation to employees right after the one to management so that we maintain momentum. That keeps everyone on board."

It's unlikely that your survey will be so narrowly focused and that your need to communicate results to both groups at the same time will be that acute. But you don't need to wait until firm decisions have been made regarding actions to share survey results with employees. Simply letting employees know what management has heard is enough at this stage.

Interactive Sessions

What happens during the survey results presentation meetings? Frehse's basic agenda is: "Here's what you said. Here are the hot buttons. Let's talk about how these results are going to shape the next couple of weeks."

Marketing communications firm Trone doesn't go straight to actions during these presentation sessions. Its survey team presents results first to the partners, who identify trends and consider each verbatim response to open-ended questions. They finalize their work session by developing a list of five top items about which they want to learn more.

The partners then hold small groups sessions, typically with about 10 to 15 employees, to present the findings. "These groups are small enough where people feel comfortable to speak up and large enough so they don't feel they are on the spot," explains Trone partner Kevin Murphy. Partners actively take notes in these meetings and repeat back what they heard, not to evaluate comments but to ensure they understand what is being said. They will read verbatim responses and ask employees to elucidate the comments based on their experiences. The partners present the top five items, and often that list encourages more conversation. At the end of the series of sessions, every employee has been exposed to the survey results and has had an opportunity to add any additional thought and ideas. "The sessions aren't 'here's what we learned, and here's what we'll do,'" says Murphy. "Instead, it's 'here's what we think we heard, let's talk more.'"

Concurrently with in-person meetings to discuss the survey results and its implications, some organizations choose to publish the results on a Web site. These Web sites can be text only or can include interactive charts, figures, and video.

The Results Speak for Themselves

The best organizations communicate the findings of a survey as broadly as possible, in terms of both audience and content. It's a mistake to share only the strengths and positive results. Hiding the negative results does nothing to improve the underlying problems the survey revealed. All it does is make it less likely that the organization will confront the problems. While it makes no sense to distribute the raw survey results to every employee, an open and honest conversation about both organizational strengths and areas for improvement at the department level, if possible, is appropriate. Though written reports may be sent out on their own or in a newsletter article, there should always be some opportunity for a two-way discussion about the findings.

From the Field
Trone Presents Survey Findings to Employees

At its postsurvey small group sessions, marketing communications firm Trone presents key findings in the form of a presentation with graphs, short statements, and bullet points. Here's an outline of their slides:

- Overview of presentation
- Who responded?

- Overall participation rate
- Participation rates by department
- Comparison of participation rate to prior years
- General measures. Trone provides the following for each:
  - The survey question asked
  - A graph comparing current and prior year results
  - A statement of analysis, such as "Overall satisfaction has improved over the past year" or "Satisfaction with the direction the agency is going has improved"
- Analysis of correlations, examining linkage of overall satisfaction level to another dimension. Trone uses a clear statement of correlation, such as, "Employees who were more satisfied indicated that their overall satisfaction was more dependent on their experience with clients than those who were less satisfied."
- Trone report card—between two and six measures add up to a score in five key areas:
  - "Am I valued?"
  - Learning and growth opportunity
  - Management
  - Culture
  - Leadership

  For each area, the following information is presented:
  - Measures incorporated into the area
  - Comparison of scores in the area compared to overall satisfaction
  - Comparison of scores by department
  - Identification of the key drivers within the area
  - Summary chart of the report card
  - Key drivers by department
- Report of top three needs identified in survey

Perfect Phrases for Communicating Survey Results to Employees

See also the "Perfect Phrases for Initial Report to Employees" box at the beginning of this chapter. You can repeat any of the general messages about appreciation for employees' time, participation rates, and summary of survey goals or process. Some examples of those phrases are repeated here for your easy reference.

Actual data is usually best presented in of charts and graphs. Follow the same tips listed in the "Communicating Survey Results to Management" section regarding phrases to accompany such figures.

Useful Expressions

- The survey results showed strong agreement with:
- The survey results demonstrate room for improvement in:
- The survey results indicate that ...
- [Metric] improved over the past year.
- [Metric] declined over the past year.
- The majority of employees said that ...
- The majority of employees felt that ...
- Most of the ideas given on the survey for process improvements fall into the following four categories:
- Through the survey, you have told management that ...
- The four strongest areas of growth over the past year are:
- The four key areas for improvement highlighted in the survey are:

Example

On an organizational-wide basis, employee satisfaction has increased. It is highest among employees who have been at _____ for over 10 years and slightly lower among newer employees. The data also showed that those who have been at _____ for under 10 years do not agree as strongly as those who have been at the company over 10 years with the statement: "_____."

Sample General Results Memo

Thank you to all the _____ employees who showed their commitment to positive change by participating in the [name of survey]. We sought to measure and evaluate the level of employee engagement at _____ to determine employee perceptions, identify best practices, plan for necessary improvements, and create a benchmark for future surveys.

The survey was administered from [date] through [date]. A total of [number] employees completed the survey, representing [percentage] of the organization's overall workforce. The average response rate for our industry is [percentage], according to [source], so we can feel good about our achievement. Thanks to all who participated.

Overall, the findings from [name of survey] are encouraging. To allow for more translatable results, the survey questions were sorted into four key components ...

By conducting this survey, _____ has taken an important first step in identifying employee engagement levels and establishing benchmark data to measure continued progress. Senior leaders have reviewed a summary of findings. In the coming weeks and months, through a comprehensive process, your managers will begin to address priority issues that affect employees across the organization.

> As a valued employee of _____, you already know that _____ is committed to being a force of positive change in our organization through engaged employees, communication, and leadership. Again, thank you to all _____ employees for your time and your feedback.

Communicating Action Plans

The most effective employee surveys inspire action in an organization. The action can be tactical, such as a change in parking policies, or it can be strategic, such as a change in product mix.

Though postsurvey action planning is beyond the scope of this book, you will need a general sense of how to proceed in order to plan your follow-up communications. You may want to report results initially, like Trone, and then report actions plans later. Alternatively, you can share results and initial thoughts on actions at the same time. *When* you announce actions isn't as important as *how* you do it. What's important is that you communicate the approach you're taking to action planning and how actions are linked to survey data.

The worst thing you can do, says Beeliner Surveys' Trombley, is to "sit on data and do nothing." That, she continues, "unintentionally gives employees the sense that they can tell you what they think but that you aren't listening." So what do you do? She suggests looking through the survey results to "find problems that you can resolve easily, find areas that are ripe for cost-savings, and identify issues concerning employee satisfaction."

Trone's Murphy opts for a slower process. He suggests identifying actions that will make a real difference in the long run. A survey is like a snapshot, and management needs to understand the context in which the feedback was given. "In a down year, employees may push harder for internal initiatives, because they wish they felt more valued," says

Murphy. "However, the real need may be for personal growth and new opportunities so they can be successful and valued. If you take things too literally, you may make the situation worse."

Whatever approach you take, be sure to describe it in your post-survey communications.

Perfect Phrases for Communicating Action Planning Approach

Announcing a "Quick Hit"

The employee survey told us that you want to have more access to members of senior management. To that end, a member of the management team will host an informal breakfast every Friday morning for the next two months. There will be no agenda and no presentations. It will simply be a time for you to drop by for a conversation. Specific times and locations for your site will be announced within the next few days. In the meantime, the survey and management teams are continuing to evaluate other aspects of your feedback, and we'll be back in touch with additional action plans as they are formulated. Thank you again for taking the time to complete the survey and giving us ideas about making _____ a great place to work.

Announcing a More Involved Process

Through the survey, we learned that the work and family program is no longer meeting your needs, especially in the area of elder care. As we have neither available space nor an existing relationship with an elder care provider, we cannot respond immediately to this important request. We are, however, committed to providing programs that help you balance your work and family responsibilities and so will be exploring options in this area.

Survey results also show that employees feel there are too many layers of management and that decisions are made too far away from customers. This is very valuable feedback as we seek to empower employees to improve customer service. Due to the complexities involved in changing our organizational structure and approval processes, we do not have an immediate solution. We are, however, committed to making changes and to that end will be asking more questions, learning more, and proposing options for new structures within our sales and customer service areas.

Several Months Later

No matter when you take actions based on survey results, it is important that they are linked explicitly to the survey. It may seem obvious to the survey team that employees will assume that a change in the cafeteria menu or fitness room hours was prompted by the survey they filled out three months earlier, but many employees will not make that connection unless it is communicated. Simply say in the announcements that the decisions flowed, in whole or in part, from the survey.

Says Trone's Murphy: "The key measure of survey success is not what you do one to four weeks after the feedback or what you say in your initial speech about the findings, but what noticeable actions you take throughout the year. It's in those actions that employees see real progress." For example, Trone's employees registered a low training and learning score on a recent survey. The partners met with employees to understand what "learning" meant to them. From those conversations, they developed a targeted, required training module that taught skills needed in their business.

From the Field
Trone Links New Training Module to Employee Survey

In the aforementioned example, Trone's management announced a new training module in the wake of a survey. This excerpt from the memo shows how you can link an action to an employee survey, even if the action occurs months after the survey.

In our last employee survey, one of the key areas you told us about in your feedback was the need for more training. We understand the importance of this need to you and to the long-term success of Trone. Therefore, we would like to introduce you what we are calling Pi sessions.

We want you to know we listened to you, agreed with you, and that is why we are taking this important action.

From the Field
Sample Summary Memo

In addition to linking individual actions to the employee survey, it's a good idea to provide a summary memo six months after the survey to consolidate all actions taken.

You Spoke! We Listened.

Six months ago, over [percentage] of you completed the [date] employee opinion survey. The purpose of the survey was to determine how well ____ was doing in meeting your needs, what new programs you desired, and how we could improve the overall experience of working at ____.

We are committed to making ____ the best place to work. As part of that commitment, we are always looking at the best possible mix of benefits we can offer. You took the time to share your opinions and preferences about our benefits program. As we reviewed our rewards package, we considered data from the survey carefully.

You indicated you want more choices in your health care program. This year, you will have new plan options. Plus we'll continue to offer our current plans with a few changes.

Many of you told us you prefer a no-smoking environment. As a result, we are creating a task force to consider the matter and recommend workable policies that the company can implement within three months. Look for more information on this task force and how you can make your voice heard.

You might have noticed the addition of vegetarian meal options in the employee cafeteria as well as picnic tables with umbrellas in the courtyard. These additions are a direct result of suggestions made in the employee survey.

Thanks to the very valuable feedback provided by the survey, we have also implemented an improvement in the reception area. Perhaps you've noticed the electronic board that welcomes visitors by name and affiliation. The electronic board flowed out of a suggestion that a number of you made. This change will help visitors to our companies feel like guests.

You also indicated that you would like more training options. In response, we launched a task force to review the options we currently offer and compare those to the skill sets we need to develop to propel our business into the future. The goal of the task force is to come up with a new training program that meets both your desire for further development and the company's strategic needs. This task force will be reporting to the management board at the end of the year, and new programs should roll out after that point.

I want to extend a big thank-you to all employees who shared their opinions. This organization benefits from your valuable feedback, and for that I'm grateful.

Sincerely,

Communicating When Actions Will Not Be Taken

Clearly, management cannot address every issue identified by an employee survey. Sometimes, there simply aren't enough resources. Or perhaps the organization is already going through too much change to absorb even more. Then there are specific suggestions or requests that are either unworkable or misaligned with the strategic direction or values of the organization. Whatever the case may be, you must be honest with employees on what actions you will or will not take, and why. As you've most likely seen in your survey, employees understand far more than management often thinks they do. Explain your action decisions honestly and transparently, and in the long run you will build the kind of engagement that delivers results.

Perfect Phrases for Communicating That Action Will Not Be Taken

When the Suggestion Is Not in the Strategic Interests of the Organization

Thank you for the ideas you provided on the employee survey about ways to improve your experience at work. One frequent suggestion was closing at 5:30 p.m. instead of 8:30 p.m. While we appreciate your desire to end the work day sooner, we need to remain available to our customers on the West Coast, who now make up over 60% of our business. We will therefore remain open until 8:30 p.m., which corresponds to 5:30 p.m. Pacific Time, but we will be reviewing scheduling options to see if we can find more creative ways to share the burden of covering these extended hours.

When the Suggestion Is Too Expensive

In response to your input on the cafeteria survey, we explored the option of using only organic menu ingredients. Our calculations show that doing so would increase the price of the average lunch by $3.50. Since other feedback on the survey indicated that many employees already find lunch menu prices "a little high," we do not feel we can make the requested change to use only organic ingredients. We will, however, make at least one all-organic option available per day and continue to push our suppliers to offer organic ingredients at lower prices.

We heard you: you need a new order entry system to increase productivity. Since all of our computers are linked, such a change would be a massive undertaking at this point. Given the current downturn in business, we are not in a position to replace the system this year. Instead, we have asked the IT department to run additional training sessions on the current system to share tips that can make it more user-friendly. At the same time, we are researching options for new systems so that we can act quickly when business turns around in the near future.

Survey results show that you would like a 401(k) plan to be added to the benefit package. Due to the very small size of our staff and the annual administration costs associated with company-run retirement plans, offering this benefit is, unfortunately, unworkable for us at this time. We will continue to seek solutions to providing you with a meaningful retirement plan.

When the Suggestion Is Unworkable

Thank you for the suggestions about improving cafeteria offerings. Although there were several calls for a hot vegan menu choice every day, we do not believe we have enough of a current demand for this type of offering to implement that suggestion. The salad bar will, however, continue to include nonanimal protein sources on a daily basis.

Thanks again for all your input on the employee survey. We're very happy to announce that we've installed a new climate control system so that each workroom can set the temperature that works for the majority of you in the room. However, due to safety and electric system considerations, we cannot implement the suggestion to offer space heaters for those who are cold.

What You've Gained

Linda Pophal of Strategic Communications calls postsurvey communications the most important part of the survey process. Attention to this area, she says, will (1) increase the chances of participation the next time you do a survey, (2) enhance employee relations by creating an atmosphere of openness and transparency, and (3) help "manage opinions" when disgruntled employees, for instance, learn that their views are in the minority.

Take advantage of the foundation you've created to prepare for an even better survey next time.

From the Field
John Frehse's Postsurvey Communications Tips

John Frehse of Core Practice offers these postsurvey communications tips:

- Share all the information. If you are afraid of the answers, you shouldn't have asked the questions. Survey results typically clarify what most employees already know. Results may be groundbreaking for management but not for employees.

Communicating Results

- Get results back to employees quickly. Aim for one week; accept two at the most.
- Let employees know what the results mean. Specifically, describe how they will change the current situation.
- Make the results available widely. Do not just share them in short meetings, but leave them in break rooms or other public areas. Just make sure to tether them or have a sign-out process so that they don't "disappear."

Chapter 20
You're Now Ready to Get Started

This chapter brings *Perfect Phrases for Writing Employee Surveys* to a close. We hope you come away knowing that although the employee survey process can be complicated, it's also something you can successfully undertake with the support of a small team of colleagues. You don't have to do it alone. You can get professional help with every aspect of the employee survey process, from design to implementation. The consultants mentioned in this book are particularly well placed to help you out, especially if your organizational climate is one that demands complete anonymity within the survey process, or if you plan to make multimillion-dollar decisions or fundamental changes in your organizational culture based on survey results. There is also abundant free information and guidance available on the Web.

If you are considering hiring a consultant to help with all or part of your survey process, compare possible vendors on the following criteria:

- Expertise in the component of the survey process with which you need help
- Expertise in the particular kind of survey you want to undertake
- Expertise in your industry or with workforces similar to yours
- Processes to ensure confidentiality
- Applicability of any software they propose

- Years in business or other indications of credibility
- Pricing level and policies
- Approach to working with you, your management, and your employees
- References

Beeliner Surveys CEO Amanda Trombley also suggests you take into consideration your "gut feeling about how ethical that company is." She stresses the importance of looking for a vendor who will treat your employee data as carefully as you do.

From the Field
Tips for Selecting a Vendor

Beeliner Surveys CEO Amanda Trombley provides this quick step-by-step approach to searching for and selecting a vendor:

1. Search for vendors online through recommendations from colleagues or through an online directory.
2. Visit vendors online and view any demos they have so you become familiar with products.
3. Using your requirements list, make a note of what each vendor offers.
4. Narrow your search to three to five vendors who seem to fit your key requirements.
5. Initiate contact with vendors via telephone or e-mail.
6. Involve other members of your team who have a stake in the final results.
7. Discuss contract and pricing details with vendors.
8. Request a time line for implementation.
9. Ask for references.
10. Sign contract and finalize any outstanding details.

You're Now Ready to Get Started

An employee survey is an exercise in trust. A well-designed and well-written employee survey means that you and your management team have listened to employees, and they know what you heard. You will have increased not only your learning but also their engagement. The employees are better off, and so is the enterprise. A well-crafted employee survey represents a win-win in every sense of the term.

And as with most successes in life and at work, one successful survey will inevitably lead to another. "Once an employee feedback process is in place," says Trombley, "new and interesting requests for employee feedback will emerge, providing excellent opportunities for collecting information that would otherwise be difficult to gather." Since it's likely, then, that you'll be undertaking another survey process, be sure to debrief with your team after the survey. Make notes about what went well and what didn't, about how much time each part of the process took, about which questions yielded the greatest insight. Keep all of your communications materials as they will make a great starting point for next time. Finally, be sure to study any feedback you received from employees and management alike about the process. Use the survey items in the box below within the survey itself or in a separate follow-up survey. Alternatively, talk to 10 to 12 people individually to see what they thought.

Employees are the real capital of any organization. Employee surveys, then, can be a significant instrument of organizational development. Our objective has been to demystify the process of planning, writing, conducting, and sharing the results of a survey. We hope that the information and real-world examples we've provided in this book will help you in implementing effective employee surveys. Armed with a few insights into how to organize your survey and a few tips about what to watch for along the way, you should now be ready to proceed. We wish you good luck.

Perfect Phrases for Collecting Feedback about the Survey

Put these items at the end of your survey or send out a very short follow-up survey a few days later.

- This survey was [too long/just right/too short].
- The questions asked in this survey were understandable.
- The questions asked in this survey were relevant to me.
- The technology/logistics associated with this survey were easy to use.
- I understand why _____ is conducting an employee survey.
- I believe action will be taken based on the results of this survey.
- I believe that action, where practical and appropriate, will be taken based on the results or this survey.
- I believe that management will take the results of this survey seriously.
- How could we improve the employee survey next year? [open ended]
- What's the one question that should have been asked on this survey but was not? [open ended]

ABOUT THE AUTHORS

John Kador is the author of many books on leadership, business ethics, finance, and careers. His most recent book is *Effective Apology: Mending Fences, Building Bridges, and Restoring Trust* (Berrett-Koehler). For McGraw-Hill, he is revising his bestselling career book *201 Best Questions to Ask on Your Job Interview*. This is his first book in the "Perfect Phrases" series. He began his writing career in Washington, D.C., at a high-tech advertising and public relations agency. For over 30 years he has been the principal of Kador Communications, providing editorial and communications assistance to corporate and media clients. More information is at www.jkador.com.

Katherine J. Armstrong helps corporate clients strengthen strategic corporate cultures, reinforce values, and increase employee engagement. As an editor, she specializes in books about leadership, corporate communications, and organizational development. She earned an MBA from London Business School and worked in Johnson & Johnson's corporate communications function for over 10 years. This is her first book. Find her at www.kjarmstrong.com.

The Right Phrase for Every Situation...Every Time.

Perfect Phrases for Building Strong Teams
Perfect Phrases for Business Letters
Perfect Phrases for Business Proposals and Business Plans
Perfect Phrases for Business School Acceptance
Perfect Phrases for College Application Essays
Perfect Phrases for Cover Letters
Perfect Phrases for Customer Service
Perfect Phrases for Dealing with Difficult People
Perfect Phrases for Dealing with Difficult Situations at Work
Perfect Phrases for Documenting Employee Performance Problems
Perfect Phrases for Executive Presentations
Perfect Phrases for Landlords and Property Managers
Perfect Phrases for Law School Acceptance
Perfect Phrases for Lead Generation
Perfect Phrases for Managers and Supervisors
Perfect Phrases for Medical School Acceptance
Perfect Phrases for Meetings
Perfect Phrases for Motivating and Rewarding Employees
Perfect Phrases for Negotiating Salary & Job Offers
Perfect Phrases for Perfect Hiring
Perfect Phrases for the Perfect Interview
Perfect Phrases for Performance Reviews
Perfect Phrases for Real Estate Agents & Brokers
Perfect Phrases for Resumes
Perfect Phrases for Sales and Marketing Copy
Perfect Phrases for the Sales Call
Perfect Phrases for Setting Performance Goals
Perfect Phrases for Small Business Owners
Perfect Phrases for the TOEFL Speaking and Writing Sections
Perfect Phrases for Writing Grant Proposals
Perfect Phrases in American Sign Language for Beginners
Perfect Phrases in French for Confident Travel
Perfect Phrases in German for Confident Travel
Perfect Phrases in Italian for Confident Travel
Perfect Phrases in Mexican Spanish for Confident Travel
Perfect Phrases in Spanish for Construction
Perfect Phrases in Spanish for Gardening and Landscaping
Perfect Phrases in Spanish for Household Maintenance and Childcare
Perfect Phrases in Spanish for Restaurant and Hotel Industries

Visit mhprofessional.com/perfectphrases for a complete product listing.

Learn more. Do more.